The Book of Knitting

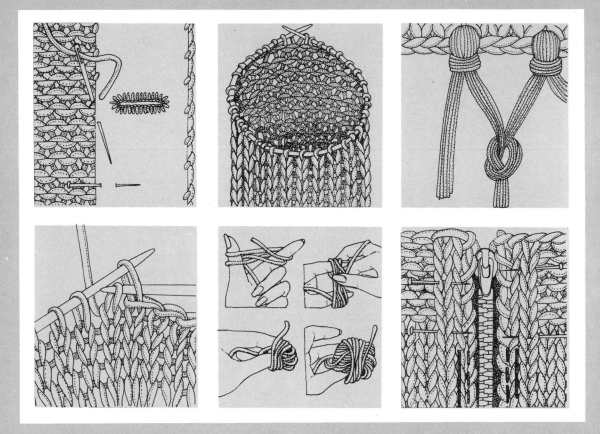

Marinella Nava

The Book of

Knitting

From Beginner to Expert:
The Best Knitting Book for You

16 colour photographs
332 drawings and photographs in colour
and black and white

St. Martin's Press
New York

Drawings by Rosaria Ligas

Photographs by Roberto Circià

Copyright © 1983 Arnoldo Mondadori Editore
S.p.A.,Milan

English translation copyright © 1984 Arnoldo Mondadori
Editore S.p.A., Milan

Translated by Caroline Beamish

Published in the U.S.A., 1984 by St Martin's Press,
Inc., 175 Fifth Avenue, New York, NY 10010

Library of Congress catalog number
84-50531

ISBN 0-312-08942-2

Printed in Spain by Artes Gráficas Toledo,S.A.
D.L. TO: 831 1984

Contents

Foreword

The aim of this book is a very simple one, although in certain respects it could be considered ambitious: it aims to be a comprehensive and up-to-date handbook of techniques, and at the same time a handy guide which is sufficiently clear and detailed to be accessible and useful to everyone. What might seem ambitious is the desire to provide something new and unusual: a book from which beginners and those keen to experiment with new hobbies can learn tips and techniques quickly and easily, but which is equally useful for those who are experienced or expert knitters as a source of new information and a stimulus to their imagination.

Knitting, of all the crafts, is perhaps the most familiar and the most widespread; for centuries it has been practised almost daily in countless households and because it is linked to man's everyday requirements it has been developed and enriched continuously. The temptation at this point to describe the ancient origins of the art of knitting and how it developed from a humble, popular craft into a highly prized and refined artistic tradition is strong. However, space does not permit and the reader's curiosity and interests are probably leading in other directions.

What are we attempting to offer in this book? Briefly, two things: firstly, the opportunity to be guided, step by step, through the techniques and ideas which, with experience, will lead to mastery of this skill. Secondly, the opportunity for those already in possession of this experience to deepen their knowledge of techniques and materials in order to exploit them to the full, and to find new inspiration. In order to achieve this double aim we have divided the handbook into four sections.

The opening section falls into two parts: the first gives general detailed information about equipment and materials; the second introduces the techniques of knitting. The former describes all the equipment for knitting including those tools or gadgets which are useful, though not strictly indispensable, but which improve the final result.

The types, origins, nature, qualities and properties of all the yarns that can be used are also described in detail. It should not be assumed that the only textile fibers which can be used for knitting are wool, cotton or silk; they also include linen, hemp, camel hair, alpaca, synthetic fibers and many others, in addition to which the more common yarns are available in a variety of mixtures, and there is a wide range of novelty yarns.

The chapters introducing the techniques of knitting illustrate all the steps in detail: ways of casting on, stitches, basic techniques such as increasing, decreasing, making darts and pleats, finishing, knitting borders etc., and special techniques. In this section there is ample coverage of a problem which is often neglected but which is of crucial importance: measurements, the pitfall and despair of many eager beginners who often have to undo garments which are too short or too tight, and who sometimes, because of the impossibility of crossing this initial hurdle, abandon needles and wool for ever. The detailed discussion of how to check the measurements of your knitting not only ensures that the finished result will match the pattern; it will also be invaluable to experienced knitters interested in creating their own designs, in that it provides the basis for adapting and altering any pattern as much as you like or for making your own.

We then come to the heart of the book: the second and third sections, devoted respectively to the explanation of stitches from the simplest to the most complex, all illustrated by photographs, and to a simplified series of patterns. The patterns are all illustrated by color photographs, and are clearly set out. Each gives an indication of the degree of expertise required, details of tension and size (with one or two alternative sizes given in brackets), the materials required and the stitches used (with cross references to the relevant pages in the second section).

Finally, the fourth and last section gives information on how to create accessories, decorative details and embroidery motifs. In addition there are helpful hints, advice and suggestions about the various stages of making up and finishing a garment, and about the care of knitwear (sewing up, pressing, washing, adapting old garments, mending etc.). This section is completed by a conversion table of European and American sizes, a table listing the most common stains and how to remove them, and a glossary of knitting terms.

Gaining confidence with needles and yarn

The tools

The equipment needed for knitting is neither cumbersome nor expensive. In fact at its simplest level knitting requires nothing more than a pair of needles and some yarn. The rest is skill and imagination. The needles are therefore the basic instruments which act as "extensions of the hands." Yet as different techniques have evolved, even these very simple tools have undergone modifications and improvements, with the result that they are now available in a variety of shapes and sizes, lengths and materials.

There are also accessories which are not used in the knitting of the raw material (the yarn), but which are always useful if not indispensable, in that they make the different phases of the work simpler and more accurate, particularly when the articles or garments being created involve elaborate shaping, stitches or techniques.

Finally, a word about the care and maintenance of equipment. Most of the materials used today – plastic, stainless steel – do not deteriorate readily, but it is advisable to take a few precautions in order to maintain equipment at its best. For example it is a good idea to keep knitting needles and pins in appropriate containers to preserve them from damp and to prevent their getting lost, bent or blunted. Wooden objects should be treated with care to prevent them from splintering or breaking. Tape measures made of plastic-coated fabric should be rolled carefully so that they do not fray.

• *Single pointed needles.* A pair of needles with one pointed end and a head on the other end to prevent the stitches from falling off is used for the majority of knitting projects.

The needles can be made from a variety of materials: steel, aluminum, plastic, wood or bone. They are available in lengths of 25, 30 or 35cms(10, 12 or 14″) and the length should be selected according to the number of stitches to be cast on. In general the medium length needles are suitable for most projects. Needles are numbered according to diameter. The size is very important because in order to knit a successful piece of work at the right tension, the diameter of the needle must bear the correct relationship to the type of yarn used. Usually skeins or balls of wool indicate the size of needles to be used, but it is always best to knit a tension square in order to be sure that one's own "touch" (i.e. the individual tension one gives to the yarn) produces the right measurement. Thus larger or smaller needles should be chosen according to whether the yarn is thick or thin, and whether a loose or a tight effect is desired.

Another factor to take into account is the smoothness of the needles; this is determined by the material of which they are made. Metal needles allow the stitches to slide along better than plastic or wooden ones.

• *Double pointed needles.* Needles with points at either end are sold in sets of four or five. The complete set can be used for circular knitting without seams (see p. 32); they can be used in pairs to create horizontal stripes over an uneven number of rows (see p. 151), and for double-face knitting in two colours (see p. 53). Double pointed needles are shorter than single pointed needles, but they are numbered according to diameter in the same way and the size selected should be appropriate to the yarn.

• *Circular needles.* These have two ends, usually made of metal, joined by a length of flexible plastic. They are used in the same way as a set of double-pointed needles; the knitting is worked around and around rather than to and fro. Circular needles are numbered according to the diameter of the metal tips and are more convenient than a set of four needles when working a larger number of stitches. They are available in varying lengths, determined by the length of the flexible plastic. In order that the stitches may reach from one tip to the other without being stretched, it is necessary to calculate the minimum number of stitches required for each piece of work, as explained on pp. 32-33.

A circular needle can also be used for knitting to and fro. Again, it is useful when a large number of stitches is being knitted, as for example on items with kimono sleeves (see p. 48).

• *Cable needle.* This is a double pointed needle, shorter than a normal needle, which is used for holding stitches at the front or at the back of the work, particularly when a cable stitch is being worked.

- *Stitch holder*. A stitch holder is used when a number of stitches have to be left unworked for several rows. It fastens like a large safety pin to prevent the stitches from falling off.
- *Row counter*. This is a small plastic cylinder which is threaded on to one of the needles. By turning one end at the beginning of each row, the number of rows worked can be checked at a glance.
- *Wool needle*. Wool needles are used for sewing up and for embroidering knitted garments. They are larger and have a bigger eye than ordinary sewing needles and are often blunt-ended in order not to split the wool.

- *Bobbin*. This is a small plastic accessory which is placed on the thread coming from a ball of yarn to keep it from unwinding too fast. The bobbin can hold several threads at once. It is especially useful when Jacquard knitting is being worked (see p. 52): a bobbin is placed on each strand of wool of a different colour and by keeping them from unwinding too fast it prevents twisting.
- *Tape measure*. Those made of plastic-coated fabric should be treated with care so that they do not break or fray. Remember that knitted items should be measured flat and should not be stretched as this distorts the measurements.
- *Skein winder*. This is generally made of wood. It is a very useful accessory which speeds up the winding of wool from skeins. The arms are adjustable and are held in place by a screw at the top of the central shaft.
- *Ball winder*. This is a rather complicated piece of equipment, but a very useful one for those who knit a great deal and who buy wool in skeins which have to be wound into balls. In fact, with both a ball-winder and a skein-winder this tedious and tiring job can be done in a few minutes and the result will be far superior to that obtained by winding by hand.

  The gadget consists of a bracket which is screwed on to the table top. The handle on the front of the bracket turns a couple of notched wheels and these turn a shaft mounted vertically on the bracket. A bobbin is fixed to the shaft and the yarn is wound around the bobbin. The resulting ball is perfectly cylindrical and regular. The beginning of the yarn is clipped on to the bobbin where it is clearly visible and the ball unwinds from the middle. The yarn should not be stretched too tight, or the resulting ball will be difficult to unwind.
- *Wool holder*. This is a container which holds the ball and the yarn passes through a hole in the lid. Some wool holders have a bobbin which prevents the yarn from coming out too fast. These can be used instead of bobbins when Jacquard knitting is being worked.

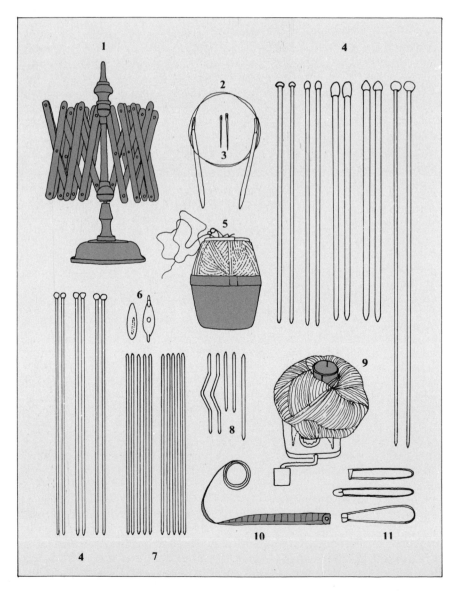

The yarn

Contrary to what is commonly believed, many different fibers besides wool can be used for knitting: cotton, linen, jute, hemp and many others. Almost all textile fibers (materials composed of strands with certain physical and chemical properties, which can be transformed into yarn) can either be woven or knitted by hand to obtain items of clothing.

Textile fibers can be divided into two broad categories: natural fibers, which can be used after appropriate processing, and man-made fibers, produced artificially using chemical processes from substances which are not originally composed of filaments.

Natural fibers are either animal fibers (wool, silk, the fur of rare animals), vegetable fibers (cotton, linen, hemp, jute, raffia etc.) or mineral fibers (asbestos). Man-made fibers include artificial organic protein fibers (rayon), synthetic organic fibers (nylon, leacryl, terylene etc.) and inorganic fibers (fiberglass or metallic fibers). The different characteristics of natural textile fibers give the following classification:

- *Filament fibers:* isolated continuous filaments, cylindrical or semicylindrical in form (silk, rayon, nylon etc.).

- *Staple fibers:* short-length fibers which are spun together to make the yarn (wool, cotton etc.).

- *Grouped fibers:* filaments of various diameters bound together by adhesive substances (linen, hemp, jute etc.).

All textile fibers undergo a series of complex mechanical processes, known collectively as spinning, to produce yarn, the form in which textile fibers are sold. Yarn consists of soft textile fibers of the same diameter, which are placed parallel to one another and then twisted to keep them together.

The classification of yarns, which are sold in balls or skeins, gives an indication of their different characteristics, the most important of which are the following: the type and quality of the fiber, its weight, the degree to which it is twisted, its elasticity and its name.

Without entering into an inappropriate degree of technical detail, the yarns can be divided into the following categories:

- *Simple yarns* (composed of a single strand).
- *Twisted yarns* (composed of several strands).

Twisted yarns have a wide variety of trade names, depending on the textile fiber used and the manufacturer. One common way of describing them is to give the number of ply in conjunction with the names "worsted," "crêpe," "sport yarn" etc. The number of ply strictly refers to the number of strands, but is often an indication of the weight or thickness of the yarn; its softness, strength, elasticity and density will depend on the type of yarn. For example there are soft yarns, often called "baby yarns," in 3- and 4-ply; medium weight high-twist yarns, often called "worsted," in 2-, 3- and 4-ply; medium weight sport yarns in 4-ply which produce a strong, quickly knitted result because the thickness of the basic yarn is double that of normal 4-ply; thick 8-ply bulky yarns, and so on.

As regards evenness of colour and texture, twisted yarns can be divided into:

- *Ordinary twisted yarns* which are even in colour and texture.
- *Fancy twisted yarns* which give special knobbly or looped effects.

Let us now take a detailed look at the characteristics of the yarns used for knitting.

Animal fibers

Wool. This is the most suitable and the most popular of the knitting yarns. Wool is the name given to the textile fiber made from the fleece of sheep and the fur of various other animals. Although sheep's wool is the most common, more costly wools (which will be dealt with separately below) are made from various types of goat and members of the camel family – the camel, llama, alpaca and vicuña.

The physical characteristics of wool which contribute to its popularity are many and varied. One of its outstanding qualities is its fineness. This is determined by the length of the fiber, its diameter and the number of "crimps" or waves per centimeter or inch – the shorter and more wavy the fiber, the finer the wool. Other advantages of wool are its softness, flex-

The photograph on p. 35 shows the basic equipment for knitting and some accessories; the illustration opposite provides the key.
1. Skein winder
2. Circular needle
3. Wool needles
4. Single pointed knitting needles
5. Wool holder
6. Bobbins
7. Set of double pointed needles
8. Cable needles
9. Ball winder
10. Tape measure
11. Stitch holders

ibility, elasticity (it is the most elastic of the natural fibers, being able to withstand 40% stretching without breaking), its luster, colour (varying from pure white to yellow, grey and black), moisture absorption and thermal qualities (wool maintains body heat and can also insulate against heat from outside).

In addition to the characteristics listed above, the type of animal and the part of the animal's body from which the wool is taken are also factors determining its quality. The best wool comes from the back of the animal, the least valuable from the abdomen and the paws – these fibers are short and do not wear well.

Sheep's wool. The best sheep's wool comes from Australia, South Africa, Argentina, New Zealand and Russia. Commercial classifications vary from country to country, but it may be divided into two broad categories:

- *Merino or botany wool:* Thin, very soft fibers, curly and rather short.
- *Ordinary sheep's wool:* Soft, wavy fibers, variable in length, but longer than merino wool. It is sometimes known as "crossed" because it is made from the fleece of different breeds of sheep.

A more detailed classification is as follows:
- *Combed wool:* Characterized by its softness and the waviness of the fleece (merino wool from the fleece of merino sheep).
- *Carded wool:* Shorter and less wavy fleece (of normal or crossbred sheep).
- *Ordinary wool:* Fibers of variable length and thickness (the wool of unselected breeds).
- *Tanner's wool:* Wool from dead animals, less valuable because the chemicals used to strip the wool from the hide harm the fibers.
- *Recycled wool:* Made from unpicked woolen rags.

These definitions do not appear on the labels on the balls or skeins of wool to be found in shops; the only place where they might appear is in catalogues or samples from manufacturers, giving an assortment of various types of wool.

The following descriptions can be found on the labels:

- *Pure virgin wool* (with the international Woolmark): 100% new wool.
- *Pure wool:* 100% wool but recycled, i.e. made from unravelled wool rags.
- *% virgin wool or wool:* Virgin wool or recycled wool mixed in various percentages with other textile fibers, natural, artificial or synthetic, to create a yarn with different characteristics.

Wool is often mixed with other fibers for a variety of reasons: a more refined, luxurious material may be obtained by mixing wool with more costly animal fur, or the tensile strength, impermeability and economy of synthetic fibers may be combined with the insulating quality and softness of wool. By mixing wool with cotton, linen, silk etc., yarn of different density, colour, roughness, weight, and elasticity may be achieved.

Types of wool. As has been noted above, wool can be obtained in balls or skeins. Classification according to weight is accompanied by a general description of the yarn. The following names are used by most of the commercial manufacturers:

- *Botany:* Fine wool, usually used for machine knitting.
- *Worsted:* 2-, 3-, or 4-ply classic wool, which is soft and produces good results when knitted. Can be used for most light articles.
- *Baby wool:* 3- or 4-ply wool, soft, strong and shrink-resistant, used for baby wear and other delicate items such as bed jackets, scarves etc.
- *Crêpe:* This can be fine or thick; it is a high-twist or sometimes plaited yarn, which gives excellent results.
- *Sport yarn:* 4- to 8-ply wool, double the weight of worsted, popular for its strength and speed of knitting. The results however can sometimes look rather coarse. Used for thick sweaters, jackets, coats and heavy knitwear in general.
- *Shetland wool:* Wool from sheep raised in the Shetland Islands, off the coast of Scotland. Generally 2- or 3-ply, lightly twisted and fluffy in texture, Shetland is used for cardigans and other light knitwear.
- *Bouclé:* A fine or medium weight wool, very curly, soft and slightly spongy; when knitted it gives a lambskin effect.

Knitting yarns may be spun from animal fibers – the fleece or fur of various animals; from vegetable fibers obtained from plants; from synthetics which are named after the process by which they are made. On this page and opposite, three important sources of wool. Above, the sheep; opposite, the cashmere goat and the camel.

- *Icelandic wool:* Very lightly twisted, soft, thick wool used for sportswear.
- *Flecked or multi-coloured:* Wool with strands of different colours, or random-dyed.
- *Lurex:* Wool with a fine strand of metallic thread, usually gold or silver.
- *Natural wool:* Undyed wool in natural colours. A thick, rough yarn used for heavy jackets and sweaters for a sporty or rustic look.

There are also various types of "novelty yarns," used for making unusual and exclusive articles of clothing. These include very lightly twisted, extremely soft and fluffy yarns and flecked or multi-coloured yarns. Or there are yarns such as Chenille, made of strands of wool knotted to a supporting synthetic strand which give the effect of fur. These are used for jackets, imitation fur coats, carpets etc.

Luxury wools. As has been mentioned above, rarer, more expensive types of wool are often mixed in varying percentages with virgin sheep's wool. Some are even used on their own to produce knitwear of very high quality and elegance. Recently certain manufacturers have begun to market mixtures of virgin sheep's wool and the fur from the coats of rare animals such as mink, beaver and chinchilla, previously only used for fur coats.

The following list gives the names and country of origin of some of the more common luxury wools, and of the new qualities to be found, albeit with some difficulty, in the shops.

- *Lamb's wool:* This is the wool shorn from a lamb at the end of its first year of life. It gives a very soft, fine and warm yarn. It can be used on its own or mixed with another yarn.
- *Cashmere:* Kashmir is a region in the Himalayas between India, China and Pakistan which has given its name to a wool which has particularly soft, lustrous, light, silky fibers, white or brown in colour, varying in length between 5 and 15cm (2 and 6"). The wool comes from the fleece of goats which live in the Himalayas, in Tibet and in Mongolia. Cashmere is highly prized for its exceptional

softness and warmth. It is used on its own or mixed with other yarns.
- *Mohair:* Mohair comes from the fleece of the Angora goat, raised mainly in Turkey and the United States. It has a silvery fleece, which is very lustrous, fine, soft, long and straight. It is used on its own or mixed. *Kid mohair* is wool from the fleece of the Angora kid, and is correspondingly more expensive.
- *Camel hair:* Camel hair comes from the fleece of the Asiatic camel. The animals are not shorn, the tufts of hair being collected when they fall out. It is exceptionally warm and is expensive. It is used on its own or mixed with other yarns.
- *Alpaca:* Alpaca comes from the fleece of the alpaca, a domestic mammal belonging to the camel family, found in Peru and Bolivia. The fur is fine, soft and elastic with fibers measuring between 20 and 25cm (8 and 10"), varying in colour from red-brown to grey-black. It is used on its own or mixed with other yarns.
- *Llama:* The llama is a mammal belonging to the camel family, living wild in Peru. Its fur is rough, pinky-white, almost 30cm (12") in length. It is used on its own or mixed with other yarns.

● *Vicuña:* Vicuña wool comes from the fleece of the vicuña, the smallest member of the South American camel family, which is found wild in the Andes from Peru to Ecuador. Its fibers are lustrous, very fine and silky, 10 to 15cm(4 to 6″) in length, yellow-red or white in colour. It is used on its own or mixed with other fibers.

● *Angora:* Genuine Angora is the wool from the ultra fine, soft and silky fleece of the Angora rabbit. Angora is very expensive, but produces extremely soft knitwear, twice as warm as ordinary wool garments. It is used on its own or mixed with other fibers.

● *Yak:* Yak wool (which is rarely found for sale) comes from the long fleece of the *Poephagus grunniens* (yak), one of the largest bovine animals, found in the high plains of Tibet.

● *Reindeer:* Reindeer wool comes from the fleece of the reindeer, a member of the deer family which lives in the far north of Europe and North America. Rarely found for sale. It is used on its own or mixed with other fibers.

● *Chinchilla:* From the fleece of the chinchilla, a highly prized rodent bred for its fur; the fleece is mixed in a low proportion with virgin wool. Rarely found for sale.

● *Mink:* From the fur of the mink, a mammal belonging to the Mustelidae family, whose fur is one of the most sought after and costly. The fur is mixed in a low proportion with virgin wool. Rarely found for sale.

● *Beaver:* From the fur of the beaver, a rodent of the Castoridae family; it is used mixed in low proportion with virgin wool. Also rarely available.

Silk. Silk is certainly the most beautiful of all the textile fibers, which produces luxury fabrics as a result of its luster, its great strength, softness and elasticity.

Silk is the product of the filamentary secretion (the saliva) of the silkworm. The worm encloses itself completely in this substance forming a cocoon, and remains inside during the period in which it changes into a chrysalis and then into a moth.

The cocoon is formed of a single continuous silk thread, covered with a sticky substance known as sericin.

To obtain the thread, the cocoon has to be hot dried in order to kill the chrysalis before it makes a hole in the cocoon and breaks the threads when it emerges. After being baked the cocoons are immersed in tepid water to remove some of the sericin and to free the thread so that it can be unwound. This thread, wound and dried, is called raw silk or natural silk. Raw silk is dull in appearance and rough, because it still contains most of the gummy sericin. After further washing in warm water the silk loses its stiffness, becoming soft and lustrous: this is known as softened silk.

Other animals whose fur may be made into yarn – the rabbit and the alpaca.

1

6

2

7

10

3

4

8

11

5

9

12

17

After a third wash to remove the gum the softest and most lustrous type of silk is obtained.

The commercial classification of silk takes various factors into account: the source of the silk and the country where it was produced, the type of silkworm, the regularity of the thread and its physical characteristics.

The outstanding characteristics of silk are the following: its colour, which can vary from pale yellow, golden yellow, off-white to green; high elasticity (silk can withstand stretching of 25%); strength (it is stronger than any other textile fiber and has a breaking strength of 45kg/mm^2(63,873lb/in^2) – relative to its weight it is stronger than steel); luster (it is a suitable material for garments of the greatest elegance); lightness; its capacity to absorb moisture; its low conductivity (silk is an excellent insulator). When produced for knitwear silk is either used on its own or mixed with wool or cotton. The cultivation of the silkworm is widespread, but the high production costs make it a very expensive material. For this reason raw silk, which can be found in the shops in yarns of various weights, is preferred, or silk mixed with other fibers. Similarly, man-made fibers (nylon, rayon etc.) which combine the appearance of silk and certain of its characteristics with the advantage of a much more reasonable price, are often chosen in preference to silk.

Vegetable fibers

Cotton. Although cotton is one of the humbler textile fibers of vegetable origin, it is definitely the most widely used throughout the world, both because it is cheap and because of the high quality of the fabric it produces, which is very soft, strong and light.

The fiber comes from the fruit pods of a herbaceous shrub cultivated in countries with a hot and humid climate. Each fruit contains six to eight seeds covered in thick, downy cotton wool, which is the usable part of the plant. The fruit with its seeds constitutes the cotton boll.

The cotton harvest takes place between August and November in three or four successive phases, and can be done by hand or by machine. After the harvest the pods are removed and the flock and seeds are separated; the raw cotton thus obtained is then sent to be spun.

The colour of cotton may be white, yellow or reddish; the length of fiber varies from 10 to 50mm(⅜ to 2″). Other principal physical characteristics are its luster, fineness, gauged by the diameter of the fiber, which varies from 15 to 30 microns (a micron is one thousandth of a millimeter), and its elasticity.

A cotton fiber resembles a small, twisted ribbon with spirals at irregular intervals, covered in a waxy substance which gives the fiber its luster.

One of the important processes cotton goes through to improve its softness and luster is mercerization. Mercerization consists of washing the cotton in a solution of caustic soda. The highest quality cottons found in the shops bear the description "mercerized cotton." The commercial classification of cotton takes various factors into account: depending on the length of the fibers, cotton is divided into long and short thread cotton; other qualities such as colour, luster, the season when it was harvested, etc. determine whether it is classified as top quality, commercial quality or inferior quality cotton. Cotton is also classified according to its country of origin: North American, South American, Central American, Indian, Middle Eastern or Egyptian (maco).

However as with wool, these descriptions are not to be found on manufactured goods in the shops, with the exception of the name maco, denoting fine Egyptian cotton, which is the highest-quality cotton of all.

The descriptions adopted by the manufacturers generally refer (again as with wool) to the external characteristics of the yarn. They include such names as *twist*, *crêpe* or *crêpette*, *perlé*, *sport*, *casual* and *fine cord*.

The thickness of the yarn is indicated by a number in inverse proportion to its diameter: the higher the number the finer the yarn, the lower the number the thicker the yarn. For hand-knitting the most usual grades of cotton are those between eight and five.

Like wool, cotton is often sold as a

Some of the plants that provide textile fibers: top, linen; above, hemp. Opposite: above, jute; below, raffia.

mixture with other textile fibers such as wool, silk, linen or hemp. It is sold in large and small skeins, reels or balls.

Linen. Linen is a textile fiber derived from the stalk of a herbaceous plant cultivated in areas with a temperate climate. It is a luxury fiber, of better quality than cotton.

The fiber is extracted from the plant by a somewhat complicated process which can be briefly outlined as follows:

The first operation, known as retting, consists of soaking the uprooted plants to hasten the decomposition of the substances which hold the fibers together in the stem of the plant; a second operation, scutching, now done mechanically, separates the fibers from the woody part of the stem. The fibers are then graded and spun.

The principal physical characteristics of linen are its greyish-white colour, silken luster, strength and the capacity to absorb moisture. The characteristic which has contributed most to linen's renown is its strength, which is much greater than that of cotton, and its fresh, soft feel against the skin. Because of these qualities it is particularly suitable for cool summer clothing such as shirts, skirts and coats, and for bed linen.

From a commercial point of view linen is classified according to its quality and country of origin. In decreasing order of quality, linen comes from Ireland, Bohemia, Flanders, Russia and America.

Like other textile fibers linen can also be mixed with cotton, silk etc. and is sold in balls and hanks.

Hemp. Hemp is a textile fiber obtained from the stem of an annual plant which grows to a height of 2m(6'6"), cultivated in cool, temperate climates.

The process used for extracting the fiber from the plant is similar to that used for linen. It consists of retting to detach the fibers from the stem, followed by drying in the sun to separate the fibers from the rest. The fibers are then combed and spun.

The principal physical characteristics of hemp are its silver-grey, greenish or yellowish colour, its long fibers, and the irregular cylindrical shape of the fibers.

Hemp can be put through a special process of cottonization, to produce a yarn which resembles cotton in certain respects but which is much cheaper.

Hemp is suitable for rustic-looking summer clothes, or bags, hats, carpets and other furnishings.

The commercial classifications of hemp are very numerous and include common hemp, Italian hemp and Chinese hemp. Italian hemp is considered to be the best quality hemp.

Hemp is always mixed with other fibers (cotton, linen) when used for knitting. It is sold in hanks.

Jute. Jute is a textile fiber obtained from the stem of a plant belonging to the Tiliaceae family, which grows to a height of 2 or 3m(6'6"–9'10"), cultivated largely in Asia, and on a lesser scale in Africa and America.

The process by which the fibers are extracted from the stem is identical to that used for hemp.

The yarn is rough and strong. It is white, yellowish or brown in colour and has high absorptive capacity.

Jute is used in knitwear for the making of bags, rugs, rustic tablecloths, kitchen linen, hats and other hard-wearing rustic items. Mixed with other fibers it can also be used for sportswear and seaside wear. It is sold in balls and hanks.

Raffia. Raffia is an inexpensive textile fiber obtained from the leaves of an African palm tree. Very strong, light, shiny and rather stiff it is sold in hanks and used mainly for making bags, hats, rugs, napkins, table-mats etc.

Artificial fibers

Cellulose fibers: rayon. Cellulose fibers include various fibers of the rayon type which used to be known as artificial silk; they are classified according to the method of production used: *Viscose*, made from sheets of cellulose dissolved in a solution of caustic soda, treated with carbon disulphide to obtain a thick liquid which is spun and coagulated in a bath of sulphuric acid; *cuprammonium rayon*, obtained from short-fiber cotton waste,

or wood cellulose, treated with copper hydroxide, ammonia and water; *acetate*, also obtained from cotton waste treated by a process of esterification to produce cellulose acetate which can be spun.

Rayon produces yarns which resemble silk; acetate rayon resembles cotton. The fibers are elastic, hardwearing, soft and easy to dye. They can be used in the same way as the natural fibers they resemble and are often mixed with them in varying percentages.

Artificial protein fibers: azlon. The most important of the artificial protein fibers known as azlons (artificial fibers produced from animal or natural substances such as groundnut and seed proteins), is lanital.

Lanital is obtained from casein, a protein found in milk, from which it is extracted by the use of rennet. When formaldehyde is added, casein becomes a thick, viscous liquid which can be spun in a coagulant bath of sulphuric acid. This produces a fiber which is almost as soft and warm as wool; it is not very resistant to stretching and creasing, but it is shrink-proof and mothproof.

Lanital is usually mixed with other synthetic or natural fibers, particularly with wool.

Synthetic fibers. Synthetic fibers are the product of the chemical synthesis of two or more different elements, derived largely from petrochemicals. The fibers produced are very strong and can be put to a wide variety of uses.

Modern industrial production has achieved a great variety of synthetic fibers, suitable for all kinds of processes and all kinds of fabric; large quantities are produced at prices markedly lower than those of natural fabrics. It is not possible to give a complete picture of all the fibers in existence; the commercial descriptions given to them vary enormously with each manufacturer, even when they belong to the same type.

The chief groups of chemically based fibers are as follows:
- *Polyamide fibers:* obtained by poly condensation of petroleum derivatives; these include nylon, caprolactam and many other similar fibers.
- *Polyester fibers:* Also obtained by condensation of the components based on an ester (alcohol plus an acid). These include terylene and trevira. They are strong and hardwearing but not very absorbent. They are generally mixed with cotton or wool.
- *Acrylic fibers:* Very similar to polyamides. They include leacryl, orlon, dralon and others. Generally used in a mixture with other fibers, particularly with those of natural origin.
- *Polypropylene fibers:* Very strong, these are seldom used for knitting yarns; when used they are always mixed with other fibers. Meraklon is one of the names to remember.
- *Polyethylene fibers:* Ethylene based, these give a very soft yarn which does not irritate the skin.

Metallic fibers. Metals, particularly pliable metals such as platinum, gold, silver, copper and brass, can be converted into fine threads and used for fabrics and knitwear. Those generally used for knitting are known as lamé and lurex yarns. They consist of a core of silk, cotton or synthetic thread around which a fine strand of metal is wound.

Preliminary operations

Before commencing the detailed description of how to knit, there are a few pointers which are particularly useful if you want to modify a pattern or design your own garments.

The choice of yarn is a very important factor in the execution of any piece of knitwear, and contributes enormously to the success of the finished article. Given the huge range of yarns available in the shops and the fact that the differences between one brand and another are often quite marked, without experience it is often difficult to select the most suitable type, if the pattern you are using does not give a brand name. When this is the case, it is wise to buy one ball of the type and weight of yarn recommended, such as worsted or sport yarn, and to knit a tension square to check the measurements. If the measurements (the tension) of the square do not correspond to those given in the pattern, a different yarn can be tried in order to obtain a satisfactory result. Other methods of adjusting your tension are explained on p. 24.

A second important point to remember if the stitches used in the pattern are altered, is that not all stitches give the same tension, and some stitches are not suitable for certain types of yarn. Therefore if you intend to knit the pattern in a different stitch it is a good idea to knit a tension square and to calculate the changes that need to be made when casting on and shaping the garment so that the measurements and proportions correspond.

How to wind wool from a skein. When wool is bought in skeins it has to be wound into balls before work can begin. This is a very simple task, but a few tips may be helpful. Before cutting the thread that keeps the skein together, put the skein on a skein-winder and adjust the arms so that the yarn is taut, but not tight. Cut the thread and start winding smoothly, without jerking. If you do not have a skein-winder there are two ways of unwinding the skeins: the first is to ask someone to hold the skein on outstretched hands; the second is to place two chairs back to back, put the skein over the two backs and move the chairs away from each other until the yarn is taut.

How to wind a ball of wool. It is important not to stretch the wool whilst winding a skein into a ball. If you should find a knot in the skeins, break the thread and begin a new ball. Unless you have a ball-winder, wind the balls by hand. There are two methods: with the first the ball unwinds from the outside; with the second it unwinds from the center.

Method 1:
Begin winding the wool around three fingers. After a few turns remove the fingers and continue winding loosely, changing direction frequently.

Method 2:
Hold the end in the palm of the hand and wind the yarn round the thumb and the index finger in the shape of a figure eight; remove the fingers and continue to wind the yarn loosely, keeping the end in the palm of the hand.

How to calculate the amount of yarn needed. Usually the instructions in a knitting pattern indicate how much yarn will be needed. If you are using the same type of yarn and the stitch and size given in the pattern, then the amount stated will be correct. If you make changes, remember that, broadly speaking, fine yarns go further than heavy, thick yarns. It would be wise to buy a couple of balls more than the amount recommended in case you are left short at the end. The weight of the ball or skein is given on the label, as is the number of the colour and the dye lot. It is essential that the latter is the same for an entire garment because the depth of colour can vary with each dye lot.

How to choose needles. We have already mentioned that it is important to choose the right size of needles for the yarn you intend to use; they should produce a soft, elastic fabric which is neither too close nor too loose. When a soft fabric is required, or particularly when using mohair and similar yarns, a larger size needle is used. The table opposite gives an approximate guide to the ratio of needle size to yarn. Of course you will have to discover your own tension and if your knitting is too tight or too loose, use a different size of needle.

Knowing how to unwind a skein, measure a garment, calculate the amount of yarn required and choose the right needles makes knitting much easier. Below, how to unwind a skein. Method 1: the skein held on the hands. Method 2: the skein held over the backs of two chairs.

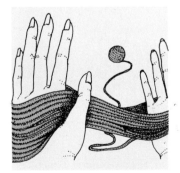

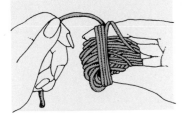

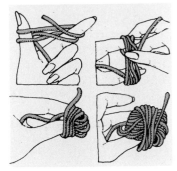

How to wind balls of yarn: above, method 1; below, method 2.

The table gives the correct needle size for different types of yarn.

AMERICAN NEEDLE SIZE	TYPE OF YARN
0	Fine yarns, 2-ply, worsted, cotton no. 8
1-2	Fine yarns, 2-ply wool, cotton no. 5
3-4	3-ply worsted or crêpe, thick cotton, baby wool
5-7	4-ply wool, sport yarn
8-9	5- to 6-ply wool, sport yarn, mohair
10-10½	8-ply wool, thick novelty yarns
11-15	Very thick yarns and special wools

How to take measurements. Knowing how to take measurements is one of the most vital requirements for anyone who wants to knit garments and achieve satisfactory results. You can either measure a garment you already possess or take body measurements.

If you want to make a *cardigan*, a *pullover* or a *jacket* you will need the following measurements:

1. *Across the shoulder*
2. *From top of sleeve to neck*
3. *Armhole (measured generously)*
4. *Length of sleeve with arm bent measured at the longest and shortest points*
5. *Wrist*
6. *Circumference of arm at its largest point (4 or 5cm(2″) from the armpit)*
7. *Hips (measured over the broadest part)*
8. *Waist (only necessary if the garment has a fitted waist)*
9. *Chest (measured across the broadest part)*
10. *Length of bodice (measured from the armhole to the bottom of the garment)*
11. *Total length (add half the circumference of the armhole to the underarm length).*

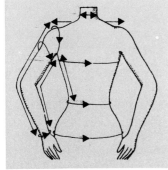

How to take measurements: above, the measurements required for a cardigan, sweater or jacket; right, from top to bottom, the measurements required for skirts, trousers and socks.

For *skirts:*
1. *Waist measurement*
2. *Hip measurement*
3. *Length.*

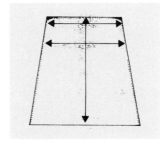

For *trousers* (generally only knitted for young children):
1. *Waist measurement*
2. *Hip measurement*
3. *Crotch to waist measurement*
4. *Inside leg.*

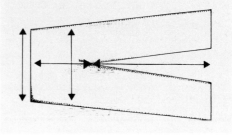

For *socks* and *stockings* take the foot measurement and multiply this by three for the length of a pair of knee socks, twice for a pair of ankle socks. To obtain an accurate fit take the following measurements:

1. *Circumference of calf*
2. *Circumference of ankle*
3. *Circumference of foot*
4. *Total length of sock (from heel to below the knee for long socks, to below the calf for short socks).*

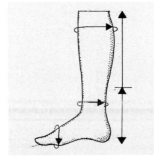

For *berets* and *hats* measure the circumference of the head.

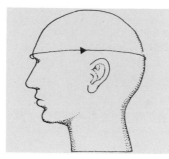

For *gloves:*
1. *Circumference of the wrist*
2. *Length of the palm*
3. *Breadth of the palm*
4. *Length of the middle finger (the others are calculated in proportion).*

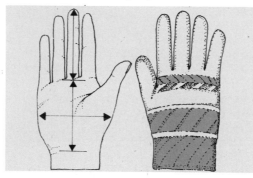

How to understand the pattern: sizes and measurements. A knitting pattern always gives an indication of the finished size of the garment. For most garments the number of stitches cast on for each piece will correspond to its width, and the number of rows to be knitted are calculated to obtain a stated length. So that two or more sizes can be knitted from the same pattern, a series of indications relating to the other sizes are given in brackets after the first size. For example where sizes are given as 10 (12 – 14), this means that in the text of the pattern all instructions preceding the brackets refer to size 10, and all those inside the brackets refer respectively to sizes 12 and 14. Of course the measurements of the finished article will only correspond to those given in the pattern if the instructions are followed exactly; those referring to the type of yarn and the size of the needles are particularly important. Also, your own tension must be identical to the tension stated in the pattern. The tension of the knitting (the relationship between the measurement in centimeters or inches and the number of stitches and rows) varies a great deal according to the factors quoted above: type of yarn, size of needles and the knitter's own tension.

The importance of the sample square. It may often happen that one has to use different yarn or different needles from those indicated in the pattern, or one may decide deliberately to ignore the instructions (in order to give a thicker or thinner texture to one's work, for instance). Since it is virtually impossible to work out the relationship between tension and final size by eye alone, it is very important to base one's alterations on a sample square.

All patterns give a stitch gauge on the basis of which you can work out whether your finished result will correspond to the pattern size. The number of stitches per centimeter or inch determines the width of the sample square and the number of rows per centimeter or inch determines the length. For example the stitch gauge $10cm \times 10cm (4'' \times 4'') = 15$ sts and 26 rows means that by working with the yarn, needles and stitch recommended in the pattern, a knitted square should measure $10cm \times 10cm (4'' \times 4'')$ and should consist of 15 stitches and 26 rows.

Test your tension by knitting a sample square. If it corresponds to the above, then the tension of your knitting is identical to that in the pattern, and the size of the finished garment will be identical too. If, however, the square does not correspond exactly, then one of the factors mentioned above (yarn, needles or stitch), or your individual tension is causing the measurement of your sample to differ from that of the pattern. The simplest way to remedy this is to use thicker needles if your square is too small, or thinner ones if it is too large. Alternatively you can compare the tension of your sample and the tension given in the pattern and use this as a guide to altering the number of stitches and rows in order to obtain the correct size, by applying simple mathematical formulae. If, as often happens, the length of the sleeves and body is given in centimeters or

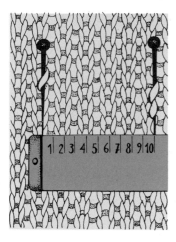

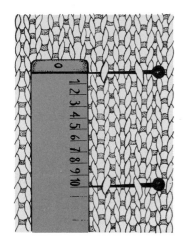

How to measure a tension sample accurately: top, measuring the number of stitches; above, measuring the number of rows.

inches, rather than rows, it is only necessary to adjust the number of stitches when casting on or shaping.

These formulae are also invaluable in that they allow you to knit a garment to your own design, without using a pattern.

How to modify patterns. Examples are listed below of different instances where it may be necessary to modify pattern instructions.

1. The pattern is the right size, but the sample square has not worked out to the correct measurements.

The number of stitches and rows for each piece of the garment (front, sleeves etc.) should be altered in the following proportion:

$$\frac{\text{n rows of each piece} \times \text{cm/in of pattern sample (length)}}{\text{cm/in of your sample (length)}}$$

or

$$\frac{\text{n sts of each piece} \times \text{cm/in of pattern sample (width)}}{\text{cm/in of your sample (width)}}$$

Example: The pattern gives a stitch gauge of 20 sts × 25 rows = 10cm × 10cm (4″ × 4″) and the instructions for the front give 60 sts to be cast on for size 10. Your sample however gives a tension of 20 sts × 25 rows = 20cm × 20cm(8″ × 8″). To obtain size 10 you will have to cast on for the front:

$$\frac{60\,\text{sts} \times 10\text{cm}}{20\text{cm}} = \frac{600}{20} = 30\,\text{sts}$$

An alternative way of doing this calculation is to knit a sample larger than that stated and, marking the area of the stitch gauge with pins, count the number of stitches and rows. If they differ from those given in the pattern, the following formula should be used to calculate the right amount:

$$\frac{\text{n rows of each piece} \times \text{n rows of your sample}}{\text{n rows of pattern sample}}$$

or

$$\frac{\text{n sts of each piece} \times \text{n sts of your sample}}{\text{n sts of pattern sample}}$$

Example: The pattern gives a stitch gauge of 20 sts × 25 rows = 10cm × 10cm (4″ × 4″), and 60 sts to be cast on for size 10. You measure a 10cm × 10cm square on your sample and count 30 sts × 20 rows. In order to obtain size 10 you will cast on for the front:

$$\frac{60\,\text{sts} \times 30\,\text{sts}}{20\,\text{sts}} = \frac{1800}{20} = 90\,\text{sts}$$

2. None of the sizes given is the right one.

If the size you wish to make is not given in the pattern, you will have to modify the instructions by substituting the number of stitches and rows required for the size you want to knit for those in the pattern. To do this, base your calculations entirely on your sample square – which need not be compared with the tension given in the pattern – and on the measurements of the new size you wish to obtain.

You will have to identify the number of stitches and rows in the instructions which correspond to the shaping and measurements of each piece of the garment. In their place you substitute the amount of stitches and rows which will give your desired measurements. In order to ascertain the amount, knit a sample square and measure the tension (the number of stitches per centimeter or inch, and the number of rows per centimeter or inch). For each part of the garment apply the following formulae:

$$\frac{\text{cm/in of new size} \times \text{n rows of your sample}}{\text{cm/in of your sample}}$$

or

$$\frac{\text{cm/in of new size} \times \text{n sts of your sample}}{\text{cm/in of your sample}}$$

Example: The front of the garment you want to make in the new size must measure 40cm(15½″) across. Your sample gives a tension of 20 sts × 25 rows = 10cm × 10cm(4″ × 4″). The number of stitches to cast on for the front is:

$$\frac{40\text{cm} \times 20\,\text{sts}}{10\text{cm}} = \frac{800}{10} = 80\,\text{sts}$$

Substitute eighty stitches for the number given in the instructions for the front of the garment. Repeat this calculation for each part of the garment and wherever there is any shaping.

This system, based on the tension of a sample square, can almost always be used for calculating the number of stitches and rows needed for a garment of any size.

Table of sizes and standard measurements. Standard sizes for knitwear are based on chest sizes. For example, for women a bust size of 87cm(34″) corresponds to a size 12; sizes should of course be checked by measuring the person for whom the garment is intended.

The table below gives average sizes in centimeters and inches for classic jumpers with set-in sleeves.

How to make a paper pattern. Paper patterns are ideal for making knitted garments when no detailed instructions are available.

The pattern is made by drawing the various parts of the garment on the paper, following the desired measurements. If you are inexperienced, a good way of designing patterns is to take the measurements of another knitted garment.

For example: to draw a pattern for a jumper, take the measurement across the back and transfer it to the paper. Draw the vertical lines for the length of the bodice up to the armholes. Measure the depth of the armholes and how much they are inset. Draw one on either side, giving them a rectangular shape.

The pattern for the back can be duplicated for the front of the jumper. The only

CHILDREN	Age	2/3	4/5	6/7	8/9	10/11	12/13
	Chest	50(20″)	56(22″)	61(24″)	66(26″)	71(28″)	76(30″)
	Width front and back	28(11″)	30(12″)	33(13″)	35(14″)	38(15″)	41(16″)
	Total length	29(11½″)	33(13″)	37(14½″)	41(16″)	45(17¾″)	49(19¼″)
	Length of sleeve (to shoulder)	26(10¼″)	30(11¾″)	34(13½″)	38(15″)	42(16½″)	46(18″)
	Neck shaping (back)	7(2¾″)	8(3¼″)	9(3½″)	10(4″)	11(4¼″)	12(4¾″)
	Length of armhole shaping	12(4¾″)	13(5¼″)	14(5½″)	15(6″)	16(6¼″)	17(6¾″)

WOMEN	Size	32	34	36	38	40	42
	Chest	83(32″)	87(34″)	92(36″)	97(38″)	102(40″)	107(42″)
	Width front and back	43(17″)	45(18″)	48(19″)	51(20″)	53(21″)	54(22″)
	Total length	57(22½″)	60(23½″)	63(25″)	66(20″)	69(27″)	72(28½″)
	Length of sleeve (to shoulder)	53(21″)	56(22″)	57(23″)	62(24½″)	65(25½″)	68(27″)
	Neck shaping (back)	13(5¼″)	14(5½″)	15(6″)	16(6¼″)	17(6¾″)	18(7″)
	Length of armhole shaping	19(7½″)	20(8″)	21(8¼″)	22(8¾″)	23(9″)	24(9½″)

MEN	Size	34	36	38	40	42	44
	Chest	88(34½″)	93(36½″)	97(38″)	102(40″)	107(42″)	112(44″)
	Width front and back	45(17½″)	48(19″)	51(20″)	54(21″)	57(22½″)	60(23½″)
	Total length	62(24½″)	65(25½″)	68(27″)	71(28″)	74(29″)	77(30″)
	Length of sleeve (to shoulder)	57(22½″)	60(23½″)	63(25″)	66(26″)	69(27″)	72(28½″)
	Neck shaping (back)	14(5½″)	15(6″)	16(6¼″)	17(6¾″)	18(7″)	19(7½″)
	Length of armhole shaping	21(8¼″)	22(8¾″)	23(9″)	24(9½″)	25(10″)	26(10½″)

Table of standard sizes and measurements for children, women and men.

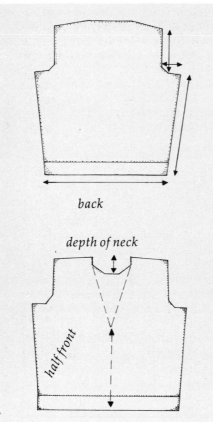

back

depth of neck

half front

front with crew neck or V-neck

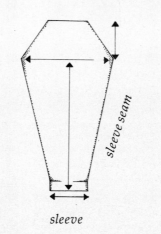

sleeve seam

sleeve

If you are designing a cardigan you will only need to draw half of the front; both sides can be worked from one pattern as they are symmetrical. To draw the sleeve, take the wrist measurement and mark it on the paper. Then measure the width of the sleeve at the armhole and the length of the shaping at the top. Draw a vertical line from the wrist to the armhole shaping; mark half the width of the sleeve on either side of the central line at the armhole and draw two oblique lines from these points to the wrist. The depth and length of the armhole shaping must be the same as those of the front and the back.

With a little experience you will be able to draw an accurate paper pattern for any garment.

When you cut out paper patterns, remember that seams are not allowed for. Add a few extra stitches for this when knitting the garment.

How to follow a paper pattern. To follow a paper pattern, cast on the stitches necessary for the width of the pattern, begin knitting and compare your work from time to time with the pattern piece, decreasing or increasing accordingly.

Remember that knitted fabric is more flexible than woven material, and therefore the paper pattern is only a rough guide. All you need to do to achieve a satisfactory result is to follow the shape of each piece as closely as possible.

modification to be made will be the neck opening which is much lower in front than behind. It is much simpler to change a round neck, which is difficult to draw and cut, into a square one. A V-neck is drawn by measuring the length and width of the neck opening, with the point of the V on the line of the center front.

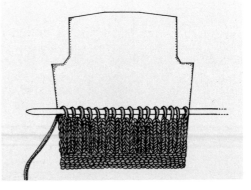

Starting work

Before you take your needles and set to work, it is worth giving a moment's thought to the ideal conditions for knitting; it should be above all a pleasant, relaxing pastime, but if you want to learn quickly and well it is important to master the position of the needles in the hands, the correct way to sit and so on, since these factors will enable you to achieve the best results.

Correct posture and correct rhythm. The requirements for knitting without strain are few: peace, good light and a comfortable place to sit. It is best to sit near a window in the daytime, under a lamp that does not glare but which gives adequate light for close work at night. The seat or armchair should have a back you can lean against in order to avoid backache. Better still, put your feet on a stool and relax completely. If you sit slouched on the edge of the chair, you may soon grow tired and give up.

Another important aspect of knitting, as in all manual activities, is rhythm, the even flow of the movements. If you observe an experienced knitter you will see that their knitting flows smoothly with gentle, natural movements, at a relaxed, rhythmic pace which is both comfortable and which contributes to the quality of the result, giving a regular piece of work with even tension.

If you already have some experience and can knit without difficulty you may be able to do something else while you knit: read a book, listen to the radio, watch television, talk to a friend. When you have a break and put your work down for a minute or two, it is a good rule not to leave it in the middle of a row; the yarn might become loose and cause irregularities in the work.

Holding the needles. As has been mentioned above, it is important to hold the needles correctly before starting work since this will save you unnecessary fatigue.

The left hand holds the needle with the cast on stitches, the right hand maneuvers the needle which makes the new stitches. There are two different methods of using the hands to control the yarn and guide the work:

Method 1. The most usual method is for the right hand to be placed horizontally above the needle. Both needles should fit under the arm. The ball of yarn is on the right and the yarn is wound around the little finger of the right hand and lies over the other fingers. The yarn is put over the right-hand needle by the tip of the index finger of the right hand; the second and third fingers, slightly bent, support the needle. The right-hand thumb, assisted by the little finger, pushes the needle towards the left while the knitting is in progress. The left hand may be used to help transfer the stitch which has just been knitted from the left-hand to the right-hand needle.

Method 2. This method is common in Scandinavia and central Europe. The ball of yarn is on the left; the yarn lies over the little finger of the left hand, passes under the third and second fingers, and over the index finger, or is wound around it. The left hand virtually stays still as in Method 1. The right hand is placed horizontally over the needle which is held by the thumb and index finger and pushed towards the yarn to make the stitch.

Casting on. Some of the methods of casting on described below require you to make a generous estimate of the length of yarn you will need. The length needed is generally taken to be about three times the width of the piece of knitting being cast on. Another way of calculating it is to wind the yarn around the first and second fingers in a figure eight and count ten stitches for each twist.

The foundation for any type of casting on is a slip knot.

Single-loop casting on. With this method of casting on it is not necessary to calculate the quantity of yarn needed because only the strand of yarn from the ball is used. This is the simplest method, but it does not give a very firm edge and it is used mainly for increasing at the sides of a piece of work.
1. With the needle in your right hand and the ball of yarn on your left, make a loop with the thumb and index finger of your left hand, using the yarn from the ball.

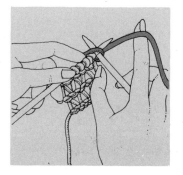

Mastery of casting on is essential for a successful result. If you are inexperienced it is a good idea to practise a few times until you can maintain the correct tension and make even stitches. How to hold the needles: below, holding the needles, method 1; center, position of the hands, method 1; bottom, position of the hands, method 2.

Right, casting on by the single-loop method. Right below, three steps in casting on by the double-loop method.

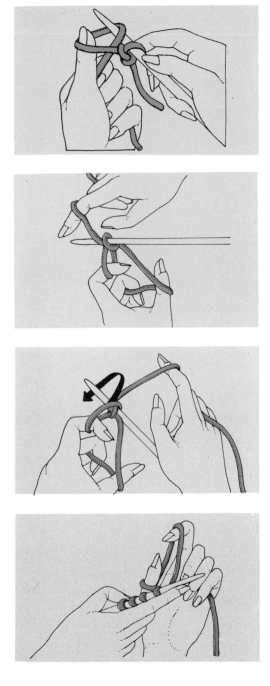

firm and elastic and can be employed with any yarn and for all kinds of work. It is necessary to work out how much yarn (which will be held on your left) will be needed to cast on.

1. Having calculated how much yarn will be needed, place the ball of yarn on your right, the spare yarn on your left and the knitting needle with a slip knot under your right arm.

2. Make a loop with the thumb of your right hand, as for single-loop casting on.

3. Put the loop over the tip of the needle.

4. Make another loop and, holding it open with the thumb and index finger, put the yarn from the ball around the needle from bottom to top.

5. Pass the loop you have been holding open with your fingers over the stitch you have just made, and over the needle.

6. Pull the left-hand yarn downwards, thus closing the stitch.

Continue in this way until you have the required number of stitches, taking care not to pull them too tight.

Casting on with double thread. This provides a very firm edge and is advisable when heavy garments are being knitted. It is a variation of double-loop casting on. It is done in exactly the same way, but the yarn in the left hand is used double; the yarn in the right hand remains single.

Two-needle casting on. It is not necessary to calculate the length of yarn required for this kind of casting on because only one strand of yarn from the ball is used. It gives a firm selvage but is slightly less elastic than double-loop casting on. There are two methods of casting on with two needles.

Method 1:

1. Begin by making a slip knot on one needle and hold it under your left arm.

2. Put the other needle into the loop, passing it under the left-hand needle.

3. Put the yarn loosely around the right-hand needle clockwise from bottom to top.

4. Pull the right-hand needle through the loop with the new stitch on it.

5. Transfer the stitch to the left-hand needle, putting the tip of the left-hand needle under the right-hand needle.

2. Put the loop over the point of the needle, removing your fingers downwards and drawing up the loop around the needle.

Repeat this operation until you have the required number of stitches, taking care to keep them rather loose.

Double-loop casting on. This is the most widely used method of casting on; it is

Casting on with two needles: left, method 1; right, method 2.

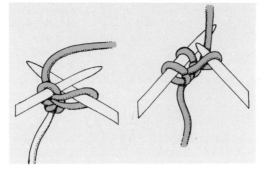

needle under the right-hand needle.

Repeat steps 2 to 5 until you have the required number of stitches on the left-hand needle.

Repeat steps 2 to 5 until you have the required number of stitches on the left-hand needle.

Method 2:
1. Make a slip knot and a single-loop stitch and place the needle in your left hand.
2. Put the tip of the other needle between the two loops, passing under the left-hand needle.
3. Put the yarn loosely around the right-hand needle clockwise from bottom to top.
4. Pull the right-hand needle through the loop with the new stitch on it.
5. Transfer the stitch to the left-hand needle, putting the tip of the left-hand

Casting on by the invisible method. This provides a rounded edge. It is not easy to do, so it is advisable to practise a few times before starting the actual piece of work. Once you have acquired this technique of casting on you can use it on any edge that requires particular elasticity and strength. There are two methods of casting on invisibly.

Method 1:
Two pairs of needles are needed for this method, one the correct size for the yarn and the other two sizes smaller. You will also need a length of yarn of a different colour from the yarn you are using; this will be called "spare yarn."
1. With the spare yarn and the needles you will be using for the main knitting (the larger needles) cast on half the number of stitches you will eventually need.
2. Work these stitches in k.1, p.1 rib (see p. 57) for five or more rows, then break off the yarn.
3. With the finer needles and the correct yarn work across the last rib row in rib, working a knit stitch and a purl stitch into each stitch, thus doubling the number of stitches you originally cast on.
4. With the larger needles knit all the knit stitches and slip the purl stitches purl-wise.
5. Continue as in step 4 for five or six rows. Then proceed in normal k.1, p.1 rib for the required length.
6. At the end of the last row knitted with the spare yarn, pull the yarn firmly. The contrast rib will come off and the resulting cast on edge will be invisible.

Method 2:
You will need to calculate how much yarn will be necessary for casting on by this method.
1. Hold the needle under your right arm, with the ball of yarn on your left and the length of yarn needed for casting on on your right.
2. Make a slip knot. This stitch will not be worked.

Right, casting on invisibly, method 1; below, the four steps in invisible casting on, method 2.

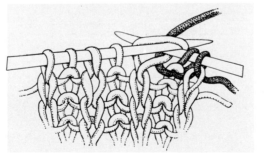

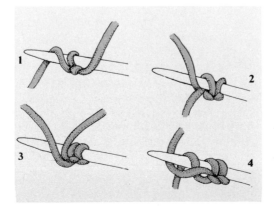

3. Using your left hand wind the yarn from the ball around the needle from bottom to top, bringing it back to bottom left.

4. Using your right hand bring the yarn on the right over to the left, passing it under the needle, so that it lies behind the other strand. This makes the first knit stitch.

5. Using the left hand wind the yarn from the ball around the needle from bottom to top, bringing it back to bottom left.

6. Using the right hand bring the loose yarn across to the right, passing it under the needle, in front of the other strand. This makes the second stitch, purl.

Repeat steps 3 to 6 for the number of stitches required. To sum up briefly: wind the yarn around the needle with the left hand and complete the stitches by passing the other strand alternately over and under it before returning it to the right.

It is advisable to finish the casting on with a purl stitch, i.e. to cast on an even number of stitches (not counting the first slip knot), in order to be able to work the first row beginning with a knit stitch. In this type of casting on, as with the previous one, the knit stitches of each row should be knitted and the purl stitches slipped purlwise. When you have completed the row, drop the slip knot off the needle at the end of the row; continue to work in this way for two or three more rows until you have a firm edge. At this stage if you have cast on and knitted the first few rows correctly you should be able, by pulling the dropped slip knot carefully, to pull the thread away without difficulty, leaving an invisible cast on edge.

When five or six rows have been worked in k.1, slip 1 purlwise rib, continue in normal single rib (see p. 57) for the required length.

Invisible binding off. Invisible binding off of an edge in k.1, slip 1 purlwise rib is done by threading the end of the yarn used for the knitting through each stitch using a blunt-ended needle. Care must be taken to allow enough yarn to bind off all the stitches.

Method:

1. Hold the needle with the stitches in your left hand, and the blunt-ended needle threaded with the end of the yarn in your right.

2. Insert the needle purlwise into the first (knit) stitch and slip it off the needle.

3. Insert the needle knitwise into the second (purl) stitch and slip it off the needle.

4. Pass the needle through the first stitch slipped off the needle, then purlwise through the third (knit) stitch – the first now left on the needle – and slip it off the needle.

5. Pass the needle through the second stitch slipped off the needle, then knitwise through the fourth (purl) stitch – the first now left on the needle – and slip it off the needle.

Continue in this way, repeating steps 2 to 5 until all the stitches have been bound off.

If worked correctly and carefully the resulting binding off should be invisible. Fasten the end with a couple of small stitches.

Casting on and knitting with a set of double pointed needles. When knitting socks, gloves, hats and anything else that is worked in a circle without seams, a set of four or five needles can be used. There are two methods of casting on.

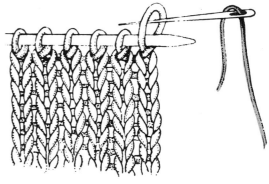

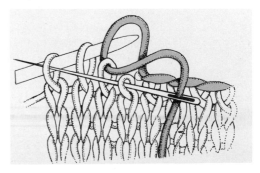

Two steps in binding off stitches by the invisible method.

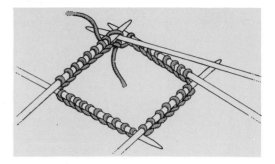

Method 1:
The stitches are cast on by any of the methods already described on a single needle and then divided between three or four needles; great care must be taken not to twist them.

Method 2:
Depending on whether you are using a set of four or five needles, cast on a third or a quarter of the stitches on one needle, using one of the two-needle methods of casting on. Make one extra stitch, and transfer this to the second needle. Cast on the same number of stitches using the same method on the second, third and, if using a set of five, fourth needles.

Slip the last stitch on to the remaining needle, and, taking great care that the stitches are not twisted, begin knitting the stitches from the first needle. When they have all been worked the needle thus freed is used to work the stitches on the next needle, and so on. The round is finished when the stitches on all three (or four) needles have been worked. Because you never turn the work, if you knit every stitch, the flat side of stockinette stitch will be on the outside of the work; if some purl stitches appear on the outside it means that the cast on stitches have been twisted.

To obtain garter stitch on four needles you have to work one knit row and one purl row alternately.

To obtain ribbing on four needles work the stitches as they appear on the needles, knit over knit and purl over purl.

To bind off circular knitting see p. 51.

Choosing circular needles. A circular needle is also used for knitting without seams and is preferable to a set of double pointed needles when a large number of stitches (more than eighty) is required. If you decide to use a circular needle you must calculate the length required to knit each part of the garment. The correct length is determined by the smallest number of stitches to be worked rather than by the number of stitches cast on, because the stitches must cover the length of the needle from tip to tip without being over-stretched. It is thus vital that the needle should not be too long. By choosing its length according to the minimum number of stitches there is no risk that the needle will be too short: four times the minimum number of stitches can be worked on a circular needle.

To decide on the length of the circular needle, besides working out the minimum number of stitches required you also need to check your tension. To do this you should knit a tension sample and work out the number of stitches and rows in a 10cm × 10cm(4″ × 4″) square.

Casting on and knitting with a circular needle. The stitches should be cast on using one of the methods described above. If a single needle method is chosen use only one tip of the circular needle; use both ends for a double needle method. If

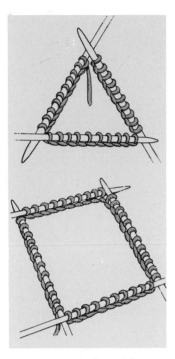

Casting on stitches with a set of double pointed needles. Top, casting on with three needles; above, casting on with four needles; far right, starting work with the fifth needle.

The table shows the length of circular needle required for different tensions and different numbers of stitches. For example if the tension given is 21 stitches to 10cm(4″), and the minimum number of stitches is 146, the number nearest to it, 126, indicates that a needle measuring 60cm(24″) should be used.

TENSION (number of stitches per 10cm/4″)	Length of the circular needle in centimeters (inches)				
	40(16″)	60(24″)	80(32″)	90(36″)	100(40″)
	Minimum number of stitches				
20	80	120	160	180	200
21	84	126	168	189	210
22	88	132	176	198	220
23	92	138	184	207	230
24	96	144	192	216	240
25	100	150	200	225	250
26	104	156	208	234	260
27	108	162	216	243	270
28	112	168	224	252	280
29	116	174	232	261	290
30	120	180	240	270	300
31	124	186	248	279	310
32	128	192	256	288	320
33	132	198	264	297	330
34	136	204	272	306	340
35	140	210	280	315	350

using only one end it is a good idea to wind a rubber band around the other so that the stitches can be pushed along the plastic joining the two tips without danger of their falling off. When you have cast on all the stitches they should cover the needle from one end to the other.

Begin knitting in the following way:

1. With the ball of yarn on your right, attach a thread of contrasting colour to the right-hand end; this indicates the beginning of each row.

2. As when working on a set of needles, it is essential to ensure that the stitches are not twisted.

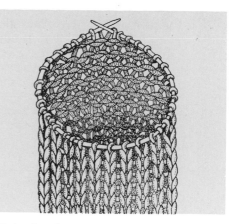

3. Knit the first stitch on the left-hand needle, pulling the yarn quite tight in order to avoid slack stitches across the join.

4. Knit all the stitches. When you reach the contrast thread the first round is complete.

5. Pass the contrast thread on to the right-hand needle and start the next round, and so on.

As you knit, pass the contrast thread from one needle to the other at the end of each round. When the work is completed the contrast thread is removed. Another way of marking the beginning of a round is to fasten the contrast thread and pass it alternately from the front to the back of the work between the first and last stitches of a round.

As when working on four needles, the circular needle produces stockinette stitch when every row is knitted; garter stitch is obtained by working a knit row and a purl row alternately; rib by working each stitch as it appears on the needle, knit over knit and purl over purl.

To bind off on a circular needle see p. 51.

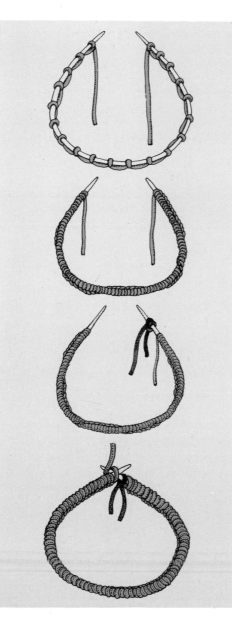

Casting on with a circular needle. From top to bottom, incorrect tension; correct tension with stitches twisted; contrast thread marking the beginning of each row; starting to knit. Far right, a length of circular knitting.

The basic stitches

The basic stitches are knit (which is also known as plain) and purl. They are the simplest stitches to execute, and a complete article can be knitted using just these two stitches. They also always feature in the execution of more complicated stitches, so it is essential to be familiar with them. Fancy stitches not based solely on plain and purl make use of yarn forward, twisted and slipped stitches etc., often in combination with the basic stitches and are an integral part of more complicated patterns.

To work knit stitches. Holding the needle with the cast on stitches in the left hand, with the yarn on your right, insert the point of the right-hand needle into the first stitch on the left-hand needle from the front to the back. Pass the yarn under and over the tip of the right-hand needle. Pull the right-hand needle through the stitch on the left-hand needle to form a new stitch on the right-hand needle. Allow the stitch to slip

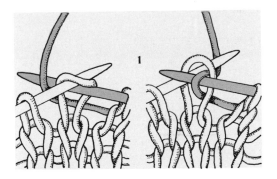

off the left-hand needle, leaving the newly made stitch on the right-hand needle.

To work purl stitches. Holding the needle with the cast on stitches in the left hand, with the yarn at the front of the work, insert the point of the right-hand

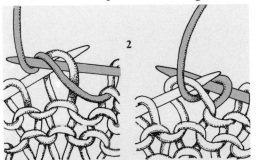

needle into the first stitch on the left-hand needle from the back to the front. Pass the yarn over and around the right-hand needle. Pull the right-hand needle through the stitch on the left-hand needle to form a new stitch on the right-hand needle. Allow the stitch to slip off the left-hand needle, leaving the newly made stitch on the right-hand needle.

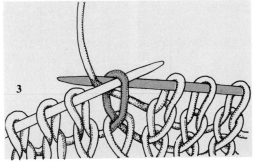

Twisted knit. This is worked in the same way as normal knit, but the right-hand needle is inserted into the back of the stitch on the left-hand needle.

Twisted purl. This is worked in the same way as normal purl, but the right-hand needle is inserted into the back of the stitch on the left-hand needle.

Yarn around needle, yarn forward. When a stitch is knitted with the yarn around the needle a stitch is gained. There are various ways of putting the yarn around the needle.

To make a stitch between two knit stitches bring the yarn forward between the needles, then pass it over the right-hand needle. Between a knit and a purl stitch, bring the yarn forward between the needles, back over the right-hand needle, forward again and back over. The yarn thus makes a complete turn around the

The stitches illustrated are the basic ones with which whole garments can be created. They are also the basis for all the other, more elaborate stitches.
1. Knit
2. Purl
3. Twisted knit
4. Twisted purl.

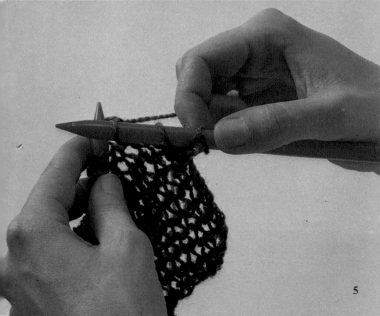

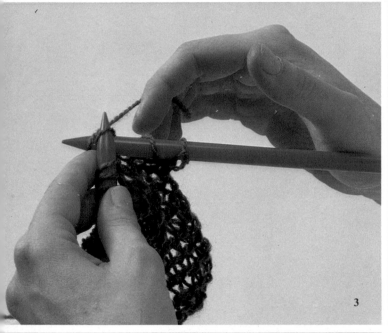

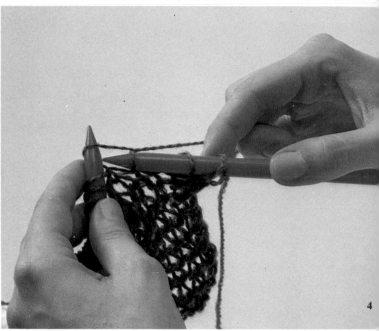

The illustrations opposite show six steps in knitting a stitch. For the sake of clarity the needles are larger than they should be for the yarn.

The following techniques are employed in many of the stitches and patterns described in the next two sections.
1. 2. 3. and 4. Four ways of working a yarn around needle
5. and 6. Crossing stitches on a knit row to slant left
7. and 8. Crossing stitches on a knit row to slant right
9. Crossing stitches on a purl row to slant left
10. Crossing stitches on a purl row to slant right.

right-hand needle. Between a purl and a knit stitch bring the yarn over the right-hand needle from left to right. To make a stitch between two purl stitches, pass the yarn over the top of the right-hand needle from left to right then around to the front again, making a complete turn.

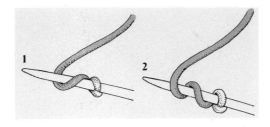

Crossing stitches on a knit row to slant left. Insert the point of the right-hand needle into the front of the second stitch on the left-hand needle, passing behind the first stitch on the left-hand needle. Knit the second stitch but do not slip it off

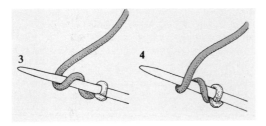

the needle. Then knit the first stitch and slip both stitches off the needle together.

Crossing stitches on a knit row to slant right. Insert the point of the right-hand needle into the front of the second stitch on the left-hand needle, passing in front of the first stitch. Knit the second stitch but do not slip it off the needle. Then knit the first stitch on the left-hand needle (the one in front of the stitch already knitted) and slip both stitches off the needle together.

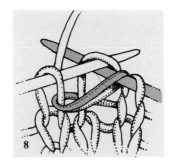

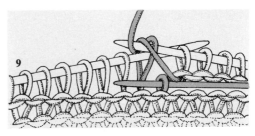

Crossing stitches on a purl row to slant left. Put the first stitch on the left-hand needle on a spare needle, then purl the second stitch. Replace the stitch on the spare needle on the left-hand needle and purl it.

Crossing stitches on a purl row to slant right. Insert the point of the right-hand needle into the front of the second stitch on the left-hand needle, passing in front of the first stitch. Purl this stitch but do

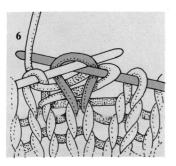

not slip it off the needle. Then purl the first stitch on the left-hand needle and slip both stitches off the needle together.

Double stitch. This stitch is frequently used in pattern knitting. On a knit row, insert the point of the right-hand needle through the stitch in the row below the

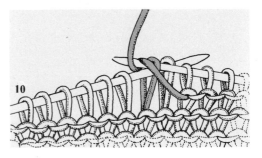

stitch on the left-hand needle. Knit this stitch, slipping it off the needle together with the loop in the row above.

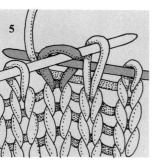

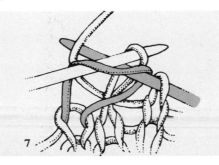

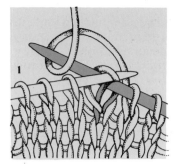

1. Double stitch
2. Slipping a stitch knitwise
3. Slipping a stitch purlwise
4. Slipped stitch decrease (passing a slipped stitch over)
5. Double slipped stitch decrease (passing a slipped stitch over two stitches knitted together)
6. Elongated stitch.

Slipping a stitch knitwise. Insert the right-hand needle into the first stitch on the left-hand needle as for a knitted stitch. Slip the stitch on to the right-hand needle without knitting it.

Slipping a stitch purlwise. Insert the right-hand needle into the first stitch on the left-hand needle as for a purled stitch.

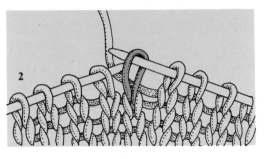

Slip the stitch on to the right-hand needle without purling it.

Slipped stitch decrease. By passing a slipped stitch over a worked one, one stitch may be decreased on a knit or a purl

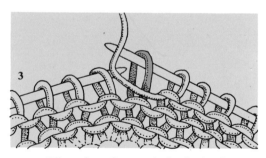

row. Slip the first stitch knitwise or purlwise, knit or purl the second stitch, then using the point of the left-hand needle pass the slipped stitch over it.

Double slipped stitch decrease. Two stitches are lost simultaneously by this method. Slip the first stitch knitwise or purlwise, knit or purl the second and third stitches on the left-hand needle

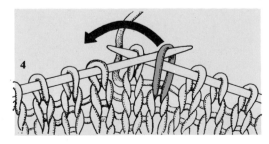

together, then pass the slipped stitch over the worked stitches.

Elongated stitches. Elongated stitches can be used to give an attractive open-work effect. Insert the right-hand needle into the first stitch on the left-hand needle either knitwise or purlwise. Wind the yarn two or three times around the

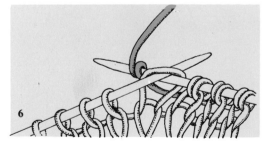

right-hand needle, then knit or purl the stitch as usual. On the following row work the stitches in the normal way letting the extra twists slip off the needle. The length of the resulting stitch will depend on the number of times the yarn has been twisted around the needle.

Increasing and decreasing

The various ways of increasing and decreasing all produce slightly different effects. The descriptions given below aim

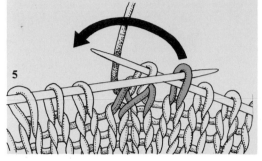

to help you choose the method best suited to your purpose.

A piece of knitting may be shaped by increasing or decreasing either at the edge of the work or in the course of a row (externally or internally).

Internal increasing. In order to shape the right-hand edge of a piece of knitting, one or more stitches may be added either immediately after the selvage, or two or three stitches in from the beginning of the row. To shape the left-hand edge, increase at the same point before the end of the row. The effect of working a constant number of stitches before the increase is to create a band of bias knitting which will emphasize the shaping.

There are four methods of increasing stitches in the course of a row.

● *K.1, p.1 into the same stitch.* This increase is made by knitting a stitch and, before slipping it off the left-hand needle, bringing the yarn forward and purling into the same stitch. A small horizontal stitch will be created on the right side of the work.

Internal increasing:
7. k.1, p.1 into same stitch
8. knitting into stitch below
9. make one between two stitches
10. openwork increasing
11. openwork increases either side of a central stitch

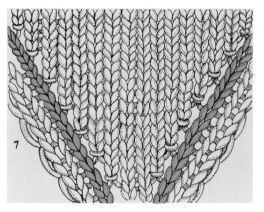

● *Knitting into the stitch below.* Knit (or purl) the stitch in the row below the stitch on the left-hand needle, then knit or purl the latter. This type of increase is scarcely visible.

● *Make one between two stitches.* Raise the horizontal strand between two stitches with the right-hand needle and place it

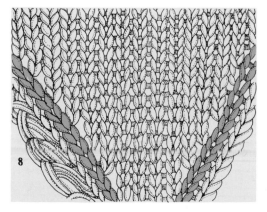

on the left-hand needle and then knit into the back of this extra stitch. Each increase makes a small decorative hole.

● *Openwork increasing.* On a knit row, yarn around needle; on the return row, purl this extra stitch, to give an eyelet effect.

● *Increasing on either side of a central stitch.* If any of the above methods of increasing are paired on either side of a central stitch, the effect of bias knitting will be produced.

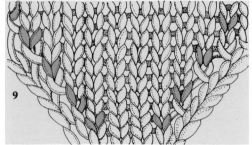

External increasing. Where it is necessary to add more than one or two stitches at the edge of the work, such as when making a button stand, the required number of stitches are cast on by the single loop method (see p. 28). This external increase is also used to compen-

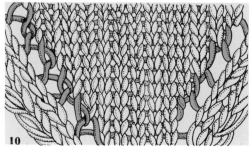

sate for bound off stitches, as when making buttonholes.

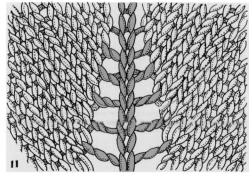

Internal decreasing. Decreasing a stitch in the course of a row causes one or more stitches to slant to the right or left on the right side of the work. There are two main methods of decreasing – knitting or purling two stitches together, and the slipped stitch decrease described on p. 38. However a great variety of decorative effects may be obtained, depending on

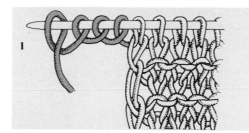

whether the decrease is worked at the beginning or end of a row, whether it is worked on a knit or a purl row, and whether it is a single or a multiple decrease. It is particularly important to pair decreases correctly when working raglan shaping or the shaping for a V-neck, where to use the same technique on both right and left edges would spoil the appearance of the garment.

As with increasing, if two or three edge stitches are worked before the decrease, they will form a band of bias knitting which emphasizes the shaping.

Single decreases.
● *Figures 2 and* 3. On every knit row, to shape the right-hand edge, knit the required number of edge stitches, slip one

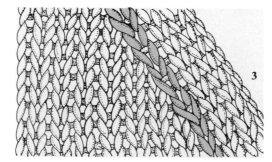

stitch knitwise, knit the next stitch and pass the slipped stitch over the knitted stitch. The same effect can be achieved by knitting two stitches together, inserting the needle into the backs of the stitches.

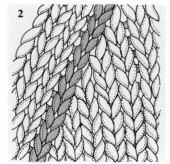

To shape the left-hand edge, knit together the two stitches before the required number of edge stitches at the end of the row,

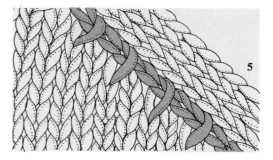

thus: insert the right-hand needle first into the second stitch, then into the first stitch on the left-hand needle.

To produce the same right-side effect when decreasing on purl rows, at the beginning of the row, purl two stitches together. At the end of the row, purl one, transfer this stitch from the right-hand

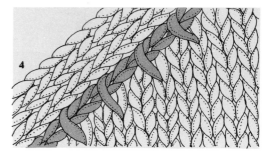

needle to the left-hand needle; pass the second stitch over the first and return it to the right-hand needle. The same effect is achieved by purling two stitches through the backs of the stitches.
● *Figures 4 and 5*. At the beginning of a knit row, knit one, transfer this stitch to the left-hand needle, pass the second stitch over it and return it to the right-hand needle.

At the end of the row, slip one, knit one, pass the slipped stitch over.

Double decreases. Two stitches may be decreased in a single operation, by a combination of the above techniques.

• *Figures 6 and 7*. At the beginning of a knit row, knit three stitches together. At the end of the row, knit three stitches

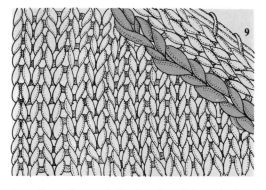

together through the backs of the stitches.

If decreasing on purl rows, an identical right-side effect is obtained thus: at the beginning of the row, purl one and return this stitch to the left-hand needle; keep-

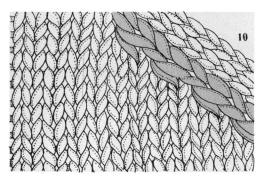

ing the yarn at the front of the work, pass the second and third stitches over the first; return the stitch to the right-hand needle. At the end of a row, purl three stitches together.

• *Figures 8 and 9*. At the beginning of the row, slip one stitch knitwise, knit two

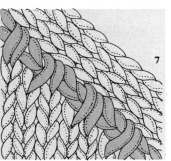

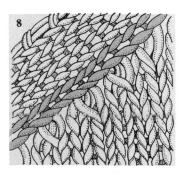

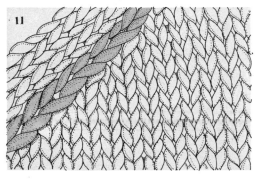

together and pass the slipped stitch over. At the end of the row, slip one stitch knitwise, knit one, pass the slipped stitch over and transfer this stitch from the right-hand needle to the left-hand needle; pass the second stitch over the first and return this stitch to the right-hand needle.

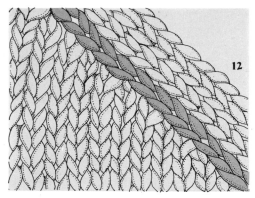

• *Figures 10 and 11*. At the beginning of the row, slip two stitches separately on to the right-hand needle knitwise, knit the third stitch and pass the two slipped stitches over it. At the end of the row, knit three stitches together.

• *Figure 12*. Rather than working a double decrease on every alternate row,

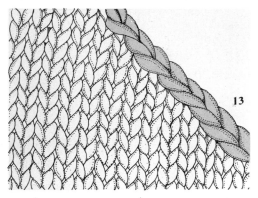

an identical effect may by obtained by working a single decrease at each end of every row.

External decreasing. Slip one or more stitches at the beginning of the row, knit one and pass the slipped stitch or stitches over. To avoid a staircase effect, slip the last stitch of each row, turn the work round, work the stitch that you slipped, then slip the second stitch and pass the first over the second.

Finishing touches

The techniques described in this section give a professional finish to handknitted articles.

Selvages. The first and last stitches of each row must always be regular and firm. Selvages are not usually included in a pattern, therefore particularly when working a fancy stitch, it is advisable to cast on two extra stitches and work them according to one of the following methods.

Chain edge. Slip the first stitch of every knit row and knit the last stitch. On purl rows, slip the first stitch purlwise and purl the last stitch.

Garter stitch edge. Slip the last stitch of every row (including purl rows) knitwise and knit the first stitch of every row, including purl rows.

The way a garment is finished is immediately noticeable and, if well done, can add a distinctive touch.
1. Chain edge
2. Garter stitch edge
3. Pearl edge
4. Stockinette stitch edge
5. Picking up stitches.

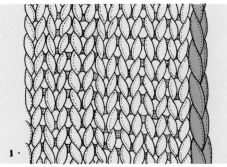

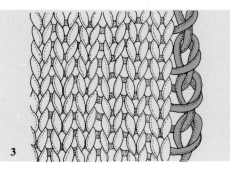

Pearl edge. Slip the first stitch of every row (including purl rows) knitwise through the back of the stitch (see p. 34, twisted knit). Knit the last stitch of every row, including purl rows.

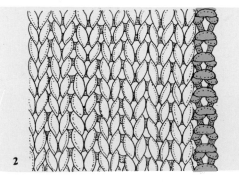

Stockinette stitch edge. This is used when fancy stitches are being worked and is obtained by knitting the first and last stitch of every knit row, and purling the first and last stitch of every purl row.

Picking up stitches. Borders can either be knitted as part of the main work, knitted separately and stitched on, or knitted on picked up stitches.

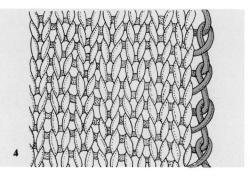

In order to knit a border directly on to a selvage, a bound off or shaped edge, such as an armhole or a neckline, rather than casting on the border separately, it is necessary to know how to pick up stitches.

This can be done straight on to a knitting needle, but the result is neater if you use a crochet hook in the following way: insert the crochet hook into the stitch you want to pick up, wind the wool

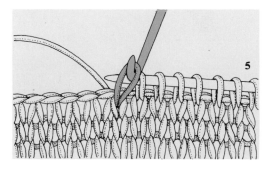

around the hook and pull it through the stitch. Transfer this loop to a knitting needle.

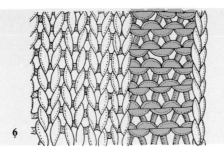

Integral garter stitch border. This is obtained by knitting the first six or more stitches at the beginning and end of each row. The last stitch of a garter stitch border should be worked in stockinette stitch (see p. 57).

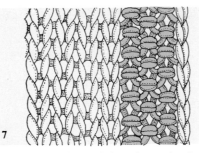

Integral seed stitch border. Obtained by working the first six or more stitches at the beginning and end of the row in seed stitch (see p. 57). The last stitch of the seed stitch border should be worked in stockinette stitch (see p. 57).

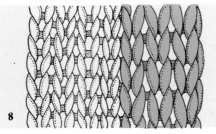

Integral ribbed border. Obtained by working the first six or more stitches at the beginning and end of the row in one of the rib stitches described on pp. 57-8. The last stitch of the border should be slipped.

Garter stitch border on picked up stitches. This is done by working in garter stitch (see p. 57) for the required number of rows, binding off the stitches on the wrong side of the work as follows: knit one stitch, transfer the stitch to the left-hand needle, *knit two together, transfer the resulting stitch on the left-hand needle*. Repeat from * to * until all the stitches have been bound off.

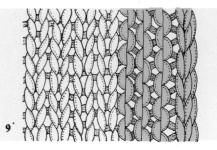

Ribbed border on picked up stitches. Work in one of the types of rib described on pp. 57-8 for the required number of rows. Borders in k.1, p.1 rib should be finished off with four rows of k.1, slip 1 rib (see p. 30) and then bound off invisibly (see p. 31).

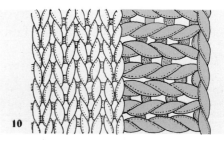

Crocheted borders. Crocheted borders are often used to finish off knitted garments. Those illustrated below are the simplest and the most common.

Shrimp stitch border. Work the first row in slip stitch from right to left: insert the crochet hook into the stitch, wind the yarn around the hook, draw the yarn through, wind yarn around hook and draw through both stitches. Repeat to the end of the row. Work the second row in shrimp stitch: work in slip stitch but from left to right without turning the work.

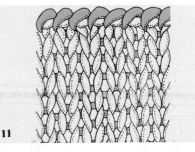

Bobble border. This is done by working one row of slip stitch as above, then a second row as follows: *three slip stitches, three chain stitches (chain stitch is worked by putting the yarn around the hook and pulling it through the stitch already on the hook), one slip stitch into the first of the three chain, three slip stitches*. Repeat from * to * until the end.

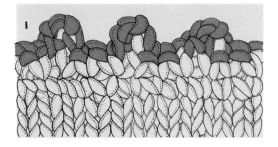

Hems. Hems are a popular way of edging, but they must be worked with care, otherwise they can ruin the appearance of a garment. There are two basic types of hem.

Simple hem. Cast on by the single-loop method (see p. 28), work in stockinette stitch (see p. 57) for the required depth of the hem; work one knit row on the wrong side of the work to mark the fold line. Continue in stockinette stitch for the same number of rows, fold the hem along the fold line and work one row knitting through both the stitches from the left-hand needle and the corresponding cast on stitches.

Picot hem. A very attractive hem. Work in stockinette stitch (see p. 57) for the required depth of the hem, then with right side facing, work the following row: *knit one, yarn forward, knit two together*. Repeat from * to * to the end of the row. Continue in stockinette stitch. To finish off, fold the hem along the line of holes and stitch it on the wrong side with small stitches.

Corners. Like borders, corners can be worked as part of the main knitting, on picked up stitches, or they can be knitted separately and stitched on. The main methods of working a corner are described below.

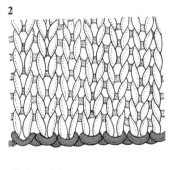

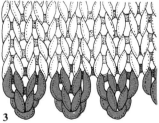

If you are knitting a border as part of the main work in a contrast stitch, a right angle corner may be made by knitting the first few rows in the same contrast stitch.

The depth of the bottom border must be equal to the width of the vertical band of stitches.

Mitered corners. A mitered corner is worked over five stitches, of which the central one marks the V. It is obtained by increasing or decreasing on either side of this central stitch, and may be emphasized by openwork stitches.

Decreasing to form a mitered corner. Mark the central stitch with a contrast thread. On the right side of the work, proceed as follows: knit two together, knit the central stitch, knit two together.

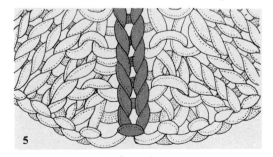

On the wrong side, the central stitch is purled and the two stitches either side are knitted.

This gives a right angle corner. By working two stitches together on either side of the central stitch on every fourth row, a wider angle is obtained; for an acute angle, work two stitches together on every row.

The commonest example of this kind of corner is the neck band of a V neck sweater, which is either worked separately and stitched on, or is knitted on picked up stitches.

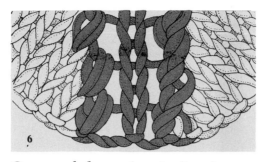

6

Openwork decreasing. A mitered corner may be emphasized as follows: on the right side of the work, knit two together, yarn forward, knit one (the central stitch), yarn forward, knit two together. On the wrong side the yarn forward stitches are knitted together with those on either side. This makes a right angle.

To obtain a wider angle corner work as above on alternate knit and purl rows (therefore making eyelet holes on every fourth row). To obtain an acute angle work the openwork decrease on every knit row and on every purl row knit three stitches together on either side of the central stitch.

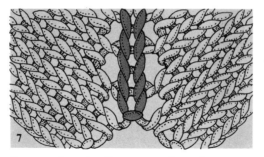

7

Increasing to form a mitered corner. Having marked the center stitch, on the right side of the work increase one stitch immediately before it, knit one and increase immediately after it using any of the methods described on p. 39.

Buttonholes. Buttonholes can be worked horizontally or vertically; their size will depend on the size of the buttons. Buttonholes are worked on the left for men, on the right for women.

Horizontal buttonholes. These are made by binding off (on the right side of the work) the appropriate number of stitches for the width of the buttonhole, and then casting on the same number of stitches on

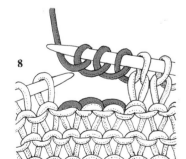

8

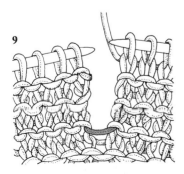

9

the following purl row. Use the single-loop method of casting on (see p. 28) and carry on knitting normally.

Vertical buttonholes. These are made by dividing the work in two and knitting each side separately for the height of the

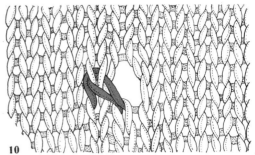

10

buttonhole, then knitting right across the row.

Buttonholes for baby clothes. Baby clothes require very small buttonholes, which are made in the following way: on the right side of the work, where you require a buttonhole, yarn forward and knit two together. Purl the following row

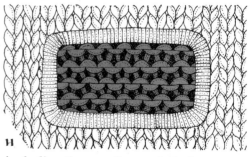

11

including the yarn forward stitch.

Pockets. An inset pocket may be worked horizontally or vertically whilst knitting the garment. Patch pockets or tailored pockets are added when the garment is finished.

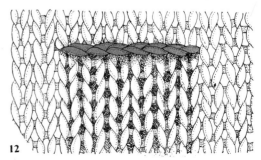

12

Patch pocket. A knitted square of the required size is stitched on to the finished garment with tiny, invisible stitches.

Horizontal inset pocket. This is worked in the following way: when you reach the place where the pocket is required, work the pocket border (usually in the contrast stitch used for the other borders of the garment) and bind off the stitches. Make the pocket lining as follows: cast on the same number of stitches as used for the border plus four and work in stockinette stitch (see p. 57) for the required depth of the pocket; bind off the two extra stitches on either side. Resume the main work and knit across the remaining stitches of the pocket lining in the place of the bound off border. The three edges of the pocket lining should be stitched neatly on to the wrong side of the garment.

in the contrast stitch used for the borders of the garment. When the pocket is the required depth, break off the yarn and leave the stitches on a spare needle. Cast on the number of stitches required for the pocket lining. In stockinette stitch, work across the pocket lining and the stitches you originally left on a spare needle. When the two sides of the pocket are of equal height put the stitches of the pocket lining on to a double pointed needle and knit them together with the corresponding stitches of the outer pocket. Stitch the three sides of the pocket lining on the wrong side with tiny, invisible stitches.

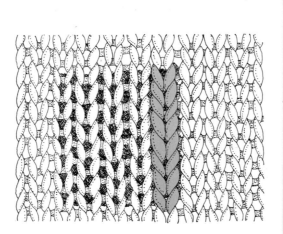

Vertical inset pocket. Proceed in the following way: divide the work where you require the pocket opening to begin;

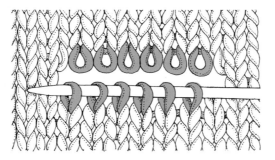

Above right, vertical inset pocket; right, tailored pocket. Far right, neck openings. From top to bottom, crew neck; V-neck; turtleneck; square neck.

continue knitting on the side where the pocket will be, leaving the other stitches on a spare needle. The first six or more stitches on the needle should be worked

Tailored pocket. This is worked on the finished garment. By pulling a thread where you want the pocket to be (see p. 148, Knitting too many rows), make a horizontal gap in the work. Put the lower stitches on to a needle and work the pocket border. Put the upper stitches on a needle and knit the pocket lining to the required length. Finally stitch around the three edges of the pocket lining on the inside with tiny, invisible stitches.

Neck openings. The classic neck openings are the crew neck, the V-neck and the square neck. Once you have mastered these basic shapes you will have no difficulty in attempting more complex and imaginative variations to give an original touch to your work.

Crew neck. This can be used with any pattern. The average depth of a crew neck is 6–7cm (2½″).

It is worked as follows: when you reach the point where the neck shaping is to begin count how many stitches correspond to the desired width of the neck opening; bind off the central one third of these stitches. For example if twenty-one stitches will give a neck opening of the desired width, the seven central stitches should be bound off. Each side is then knitted separately as follows. Bind off two stitches at the neck edge on every second row until half the total number of stitches calculated for the neck opening has been bound off. To finish a crew neck, pick up and knit the stitches from the front and back on a set of four needles and work the required number of rows in your chosen edging stitch.

V-neck. The classic neck opening for sportswear. A V-neck is worked as follows: when you reach the point where the neck shaping is to begin, calculate how many stitches correspond to the desired width of the neck opening at its widest point; bind off the central stitch. Each side is then knitted separately: bind off one stitch at the neck edge every four rows until the number of stitches calculated has been bound off.

To finish a V-neck, pick up and knit the stitches at the front and back, decreasing one stitch on every row on either side of the stitch in the center of the V.

Square neck. This is made by binding off the total number of stitches for the neck opening on one row and knitting each side separately without further shaping to the shoulders.

To finish a square neck pick up and knit the stitches from the front and back on a set of four needles and work the required number of rows, working mitered corners as described on p. 44.

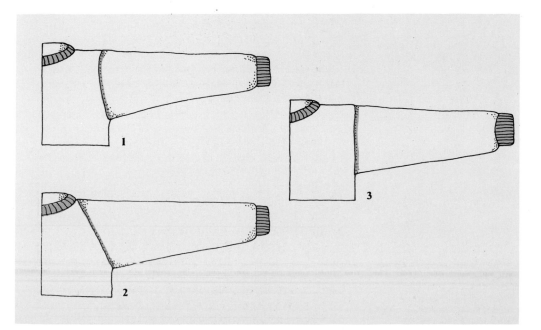

Armhole shapings:
1. Set-in sleeve
2. Raglan sleeve
3. Dropped shoulder.

Turtleneck. The turtleneck is a variation of the crew neck. It is worked exactly like a crew neck but the neckband is knitted in rib to the length required and folded over when bound off.

Sleeves. Sleeves are generally knitted from the cuff upwards; the cuff must be fairly elastic. When knitting the sleeves, increase one stitch at each end of the row every 3-4cm(1-1½") until the desired sleeve length to the armhole is reached.

Armhole shaping for set-in sleeves. Both the front and the back of the work should be shaped at armhole level, binding off three stitches, then two stitches, then one stitch at the beginning and end of alternate rows. Continue knitting without further shaping until the shoulders are reached.

For the armhole shaping on the sleeve, bind off three stitches at the beginning and end of one row; then bind off one stitch at the beginning and end of alternate rows until a quarter of the original number of stitches are left. Bind off the remaining stitches.

On larger sizes where a deeper armhole is required, increase the number of stitches bound off at the beginning of the armhole shaping, remembering that the front, back and sleeve shaping should all match.

Raglan shaping. Raglan shaping is worked on the front and back of a piece of work from the armhole. Make a note of the number of stitches, then bind off three stitches, then two stitches at the beginning and end of alternate rows. Continue by decreasing one stitch at the beginning and end of alternate rows until you reach the point where the neck shaping should begin. Shape the neck, continuing to decrease at the armhole edge until no stitches remain.

Raglan sleeves are shaped as follows: when the desired sleeve length to the armhole is reached, bind off three stitches, then two stitches at the beginning and end of alternate rows. Continue by decreasing one stitch at the beginning and end of alternate rows until the shaping measures the same as the raglan shaping on the front and the back. There should

be six or eight stitches left on the needle which should be bound off together.

An attractive effect can be gained if

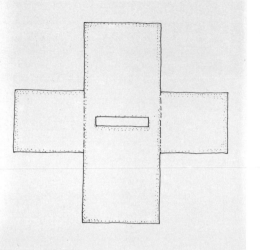

raglan shaping is worked with one of the fancy methods of decreasing described on pp. 39-41, taking care to match the decreases at the beginning and end of the rows.

Dropped shoulders. The front and back are knitted as a straight piece without any armhole shaping.

All the sleeve stitches are bound off on one row when the desired sleeve length is reached.

Kimono sleeves. Unlike the other types of sleeves kimono sleeves are knitted in one piece with the front and the back.

This may be done in two ways: by starting from the front or the back, or by starting from the cuff.

To knit a garment with kimono sleeves using the first method, work the front to armhole level; at the beginning and end of alternate rows increase two stitches once and three stitches once. Using the single-loop method of casting on (see p. 28), cast on at the beginning of the next two rows the number of stitches required for the length of the sleeve. Continue working until the neck is reached, making a note of the number of rows. Work the neck opening in the center and continue for the same number of rows. Bind off the sleeve stitches, then three and two stitches on alternate rows at the armhole edge; finish the back.

To knit a garment with kimono sleeves using the second method, proceed in the same way but begin at the cuff. Cast on

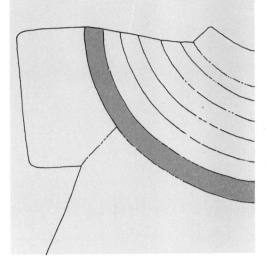

the required number of stitches for the front and back when the sleeve is the desired length at the underarm.

It makes the work easier if you change to a circular needle when you cast on the extra stitches, as explained on pp. 32-3. Choose a needle of the appropriate length and work to and fro thus: take the right-hand end of the circular needle and work one row. Take the end of the needle with the stitches on it in your left hand, wrong side towards you. Work the next row in purl from the left-hand tip of the needle to the right-hand tip. Turn the work and knit across. Continue for the required number of rows.

Shaping for a round yoke. A round yoke looks attractive and is particularly suit-

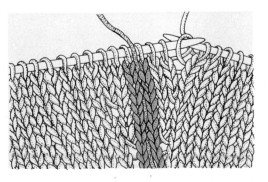

able for first size baby clothes, but it is not as simple to knit as other shapes.

To knit a yoke, work the front, back and sleeves to the underarm, leaving each piece on a spare needle. Arrange the stitches of all the pieces on a set of four needles and work in rounds, or back and forth if the garment has a back or front opening. Stitches are decreased for the neck either at regular intervals every second or fourth row, or at the point where the sleeves meet the front and the back.

Darts. Vertical or horizontal darts are used to shape garments (at bust or hips for example).

Vertical darts. Vertical darts used to decrease the width of a garment are

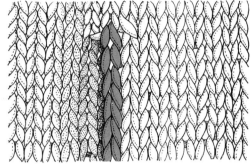

worked as follows: mark the central stitch of the dart with a contrast thread and decrease (see p. 40) the stitch preceding and following the marked stitch every two, four or more rows depending on the depth and length of the dart required. The decreases can also be made every third row, on knit and purl rows alternately.

To increase the width of the garment, work as above but increase (see pp. 38-9) instead of decreasing on both sides of the central stitch.

Horizontal darts. These are used to make one edge of a piece of work longer than the other, for instance to provide bust shaping.

At the point where the dart is required, leave three or four stitches at the armhole edge unworked. Turn and knit the return row. On the next row, again leave three or four stitches unworked at the end and turn. Repeat as necessary. When the required depth of dart has been obtained, knit across all stitches.

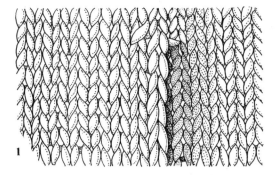

Pleats. Pleats are complicated to knit mainly because of the difficulty of working out how many stitches to cast on. It is essential to knit a sample before starting work. Various kinds of pleats can be made: flat pleats lying to the right or left, box pleats and sunray pleats.

Flat pleats. These are worked as follows. The outside fold of the pleat is obtained by slipping a stitch knitwise; the inside of the pleat by purling one stitch. The number of stitches worked between these two stitches will determine the depth of the pleat.

Pleats five stitches deep lying to the left are knitted thus:
Row 1. *slip 1 knitwise, k.5, p.1, k.11*.
Row 2. *p.11, k.1, p.6*.

Repeat these two rows for the required length; then finish the pleats with right side facing as follows:

*Put the slipped stitch and the five knit

stitches on one spare needle and put the purl stitch and the following five knit stitches on another. Holding the needles parallel in your left hand, work three stitches together, one from each needle*. Repeat the process from * to * to finish each pleat.

For pleats lying to the right, the method is the same but is worked as follows:
Row 1. *p.1, k.5, slip 1 knitwise, k.11*.
Row 2. *p.17, k.1*.

Repeat these two rows for the desired length and finish the pleats as described for pleats lying to the left.

Box pleats. These are worked in the same

way as flat pleats; a pleat lying to the left is followed by a right-hand one in such a way that the distance between them equals double the depth of the pleat (in stitches) plus two.

To knit pleats five stitches deep proceed as follows:
Row 1. *k.5, slip 1 knitwise, k.5, p.1, k.12, p.1, k.5, slip 1 knitwise, k.5*.
Row 2. *p.11, k.1, p.12, k.1, p.11*.

Close the pleats as described for flat pleats.

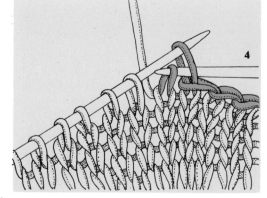

Sunray pleats. Commencing at the lower edge of a skirt, these are knitted as follows: knit eight to ten stitches, purl three; every eight to ten rows with right side facing knit two stitches together immediately before the three purl stitches. Continue in this way for the required length. Alternatively begin at the waist and increase at regular intervals.

Binding off. Binding off is done on the final row which finishes a piece of knitting and fastens the stitches. It is important to keep the yarn fairly loose to give

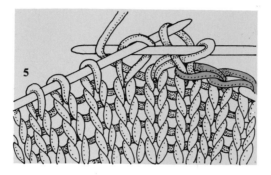

an elastic edge to the work. Instructions for a variety of methods, some more complicated than others, are given below.

Method 1:
This is the standard method: knit (or purl) the first two stitches and pass the first over the second, then knit (or purl) a third stitch, pass the second over the third and so on to the end of the row. Knit stitches should be knitted and purl stitches purled, as they appear on the needle.

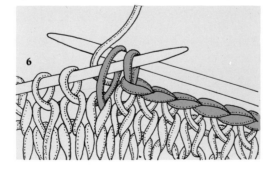

Method 2:
This should be used if your tension is tight, or when a soft and stretchy edge is required.

Work two stitches, *pass the first over the second using the tip of the left-hand needle. Without slipping this loop off the left-hand needle, insert the right-hand needle into the next stitch and when that has been worked let the bound off stitch fall off the left-hand needle*. Repeat from

* to * until all the stitches have been bound off.

Method 3:
This is worked as follows: knit the first two stitches of the row together through the back of the loop (see p. 34, twisted knit). Return the stitch obtained to the left-hand needle and knit it together with the next stitch through the back of the loop; transfer the resulting stitch back to the left-hand needle. Continue until all stitches have been worked.

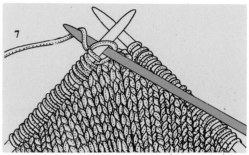

Binding off with four needles. With the spare needle work two stitches from the first needle; lift the first over the second using the tip of the left-hand needle; knit another stitch and pass the previous one over it. Continue until there is only one stitch left on the right-hand needle, then begin on the second needle, and so on until all the stitches have been bound off.

Binding off with a circular needle. Start binding off at the beginning of a round as follows: work the first two stitches, pass the first over the second, work the third and pass the second over. Continue until all the stitches have been bound off.

Special techniques

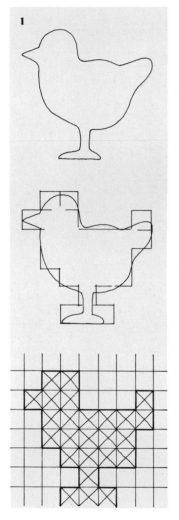

Jacquard knitting. This is worked in stockinette stitch; motifs are worked in different colours contrasting with the background and give very striking effects. It is, however, not easy to do, in that you have to know how to follow the pattern, change colours, and most difficult of all, keep an even tension.

Motifs are provided, or designed if you invent them yourself, on graph paper; each square corresponds to one stitch, each horizontal line of squares to one row and each symbol indicates a different colour. Usually the background colour is represented by the empty squares.

If the rows are to be worked to and fro the colour chart is read from the bottom, from right to left for the first row; the second row on the chart, the purl row, is followed from left to right. The whole chart is read thus, knitting the odd-numbered rows from right to left and purling the even-numbered rows from left to right.

If you are working in rounds with a set of needles or a circular needle read each row of the chart from right to left, knitting every row. Obviously it is easiest to follow a simple chart with few colours.

If only two colours are used per row and the pattern does not require more than four or five stitches to be worked per colour, the strand of yarn not in use is simply passed along the back of the work; care should be taken not to pull it too tight as this would pull the motif on the right side out of shape. For inexperienced knitters and those whose tension is uneven it is advisable to carry the yarn very loosely at the back of the work to avoid spoiling the right side.

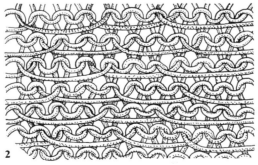

On knit rows the strands are carried behind the work. As figure 3 shows, the right hand guides the main colour, while the left hand holds the contrast yarn to the left, below the stitches being worked. When using the contrast yarn, keep the main colour in your right hand and hold it above the stitches being worked.

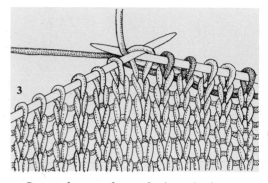

On purl rows the technique is the same but the yarns are held at the front of the work.

If there are more than two colours being worked, or if the pattern requires

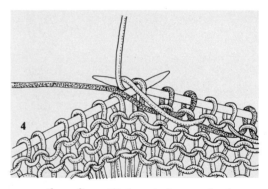

more than five stitches to be worked as a block of colour, it is not a good idea to carry the strands along on the wrong side because the loops will be too long. The strands should be woven in at the back of the work as follows: on a knit row, hold the yarns at the back of the work and knit the first stitch, holding the colour being used in your right hand and the other

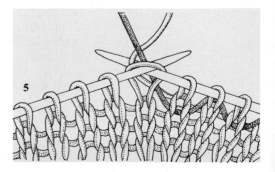

colours in your left; the other colours should be placed over the first colour, as shown in figure 5. The second stitch is knitted in the same way as the first but the

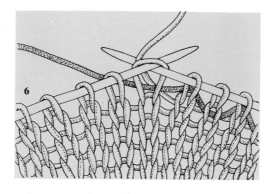

colours not in use should be placed under the first colour as shown in figure 6. Continue the row in this way, altering the position of the colours not in use on every stitch.

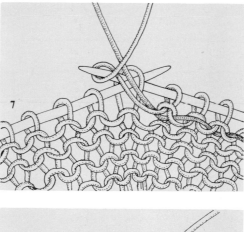

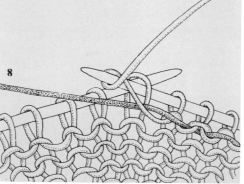

7. and 8. Weaving in colours on a purl row, step 1 and step 2
9. Correct tension for woven-in strands
10. Incorrect tension for woven-in strands.

On a purl row work in the same way, but hold the strands in front of the work, placing the colour not being used above and below the first colour as shown in figures 7 and 8.

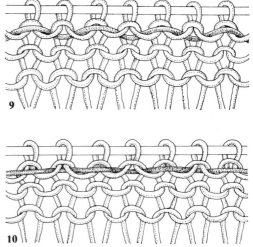

When the colours are being woven in, the tension is still very important; the woven strands must not be pulled too tight. Figure 9 illustrates the correct tension for woven-in strands, whereas figure 10 shows strands pulled too tight.

Double-face knitting. Double-face knitting requires experience and precision; it is advisable to knit several samples before embarking on a full-scale piece of work. The finished piece of work is reversible, with the right side of stockinette stitch on both sides.

Double-face knitting is joined at the bottom and at the sides, and open at the top. If the two colours are bound off together the top may be joined also; if they are bound off separately the result will be in the shape of a bag. Because the work is double, double-face knitting is heavy and warm, suitable above all for coats and jackets but also scarves, cot covers etc. The yarn used should not be too thick and bulky.

Double-face knitting is worked with two double pointed needles; two colours are used, worked separately. Proceed as follows:

1. On one needle cast on double the number of stitches required (an even number) with one of the two colours (referred to henceforth as colour 1).
2. With the second colour (referred to as colour 2) work the first row: *k.1, yarn forward, slip 1 purlwise, yarn back, k.1*.
3. Without turning the work, starting

Double-face knitting.
1. Casting on
2. Crossing strands at the end of the row
3. Closed binding off
4. Open binding off
5. The finished piece of double-face knitting.

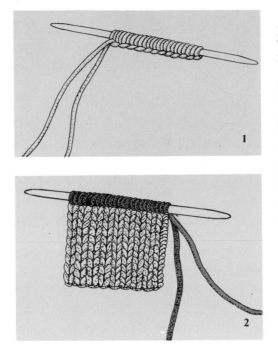

1

2

It is important to remember always to pass the colours one under the other at the edge of the work to prevent holes forming.

If a completely closed piece of work is required, bind off all the stitches with colour 2, knitting all the knit stitches worked with colour 2 and purling all the stitches worked with colour 1. If a bag shape is required, bind the two colours off separately: transfer the stitches in colour 1 to another needle and bind them off purlwise with the same colour. Then with colour 2 bind off knitwise the stitches worked with colour 2.

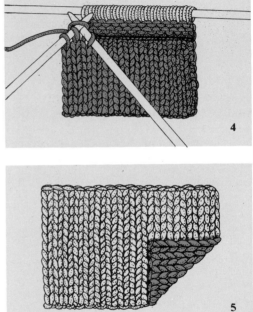

4

5

from the other end of the needle, work the second row with colour 1: *with the yarn at the back of the work, slip 1 purlwise, yarn forward, p.1*. Repeat from * to * to the end of the row.

4. Turn the work in the normal way as when knitting with two needles. Colours 1 and 2 will be at the right-hand edge.

5. Pass colour 2 under colour 1 and work row three with colour 2: *with yarn at the back of the work, slip 1 purlwise, yarn forward, p.1*. Repeat from * to * to the end of the row.

6. Without turning the work, beginning from the opposite end of the needle with colour 1, work row four in the same way as row one.

7. Work these four rows for the required length, ending with row four.

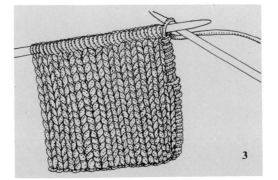

3

A variety of stitches

The stitches

Garter stitch

Garter stitch is the simplest stitch to work. It is effective both when worked in sport or bulky yarn to make thick jackets or sweaters, and when worked in fine, soft wool or in mohair to make elegant garments which need to be very soft and light. Garter stitch is worked by knitting every stitch. If an extra strong edge is needed, for the border of a heavy sweater for example, work each row in twisted knit by knitting through the back of each stitch. This gives an exceptionally firm edge. Garter stitch is the same on both sides of the work.

Garter stitch

Stockinette stitch

Stockinette stitch is the classic stitch for knitwear and the most frequently employed because it is suitable for a wide variety of garments and for all kinds of yarn. It is worked by knitting one row and purling the next, and repeating these two rows.

The term reversed stockinette stitch is sometimes used, but this is not in fact a different stitch; it indicates that the purl side of stockinette stitch is to be treated as the right side.

Twisted stockinette stitch

Row 1: knit across, working into the back of every stitch.

Row 2: purl.
Repeat rows 1 and 2.

Stockinette stitch

Twisted stockinette stitch

Single rib

Cast on an even number of stitches.
Row 1: *k.1, p.1*
Row 2 and following rows: *k.1 on the

knit stitch of the previous row, p.1 on the purl stitch of the previous row*.

Row 1: knit.
Row 2: *p.1, k.1 into the stitch below*, ending with p.1, k.1.
Repeat rows 1 and 2.

Single rib

Double rib
Cast on a multiple of 4 stitches.
Row 1: *k2, p.2*.
Row 2 and following rows: work each stitch as it appears on the needle, knitting over knit stitches, purling over purl stitches.

Fisherman's rib

Twisted rib
This is a variation on single rib.
Cast on an even number of stitches.
Row 1: *k.1 into the back of the stitch, p.1*.

Double rib

Fisherman's rib
Cast on an even number of stitches.

Twisted rib

58

Row 2: work each stitch as it appears on the needle, knitting into the back of each knit stitch.

Oblique rib
Cast on a multiple of 4 stitches.
Row 1: *k.2, p.2*.
Row 2 and even rows: work each stitch as it appears on the needle, knitting over a knit stitch, purling over a purl stitch.
Row 3: *k.1, p.2, k.1*.
Row 5: *p.2, k.2*.
Row 7: *p.1, k.2, p.1*.
Repeat rows 1-8.

Chequer stitch

Oblique rib

Seed stitch

Chequer stitch
Cast on a multiple of 4 stitches.
Rows 1, 3 and 5: *k.4, p.4*.
Rows 2, 4 and 6: work each stitch as it appears on the needle, knitting the knit stitches and purling the purl stitches.
Row 7: reverse the design, working 4 purl stitches over the 4 knit stitches and 4 knit stitches over the 4 purl stitches of the previous row.
Rows 8-12: work each stitch as it appears on the needle.
Row 13: repeat from Row 1.

Seed stitch
Cast on an even number of stitches.
Row 1: *k.1, p.1*.
Row 2: *work a purl stitch over each knit stitch and a knit stitch over each purl stitch of the previous row*.
Row 3: repeat from Row 1.

Double seed stitch

Row 1: *k.1, p.1*.
Row 2 and even rows: work each stitch as it appears on the needle.
Row 3: *p.1, k.1*.

Double seed stitch

Row 5: repeat from Row 1.

Mat stitch

Cast on an odd number of stitches.
Row 1: purl.
Row 2 (right side of work): k.1 *slip 1 knitwise, k.1, yarn forward, pass the slipped stitch over the 2 following stitches* k.2.
Row 3: p.1 *slip 1 purlwise, p.1, yarn around needle, pass the slipped stitch over the two following stitches*.
Row 4: repeat from Row 2.

Beehive stitch

Cast on an even number of stitches.
Row 1: knit.
Row 2: knit.
Row 3: *k.1, k.1 into the stitch below*.
Row 4: *with the right-hand needle pick up the upper of the two loops lying below the stitch and knit it with the stitch on the needle, k.1*.
Row 5: *k.1 into the stitch below, k.1*.
Row 6: *k.1, with the right-hand needle pick up the upper of the two loops lying below the next stitch and knit it with the stitch on the needle.
Repeat Rows 3-6.

Beehive stitch

Mat stitch

Woven stitch

Cast on an even number of stitches.
Row 1: *k.1, yarn forward, slip 1 purlwise, yarn back*.

60

Row 2: *p.1, yarn back, slip 1 purlwise, yarn forward*.
Row 3: repeat from Row 1.

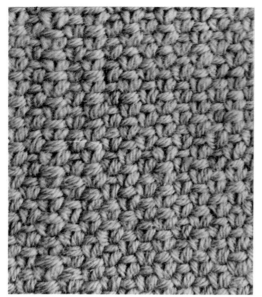

Woven stitch

Basket stitch
Cast on a multiple of 8 stitches.
Row 1: knit.
Row 2 and even rows: purl.
Row 3: k.2, *slip 2 stitches on to a cable needle and leave at the back of the work, k.2, knit the 2 stitches on the cable

Basket stitch

needle*, k.2.
Row 5: *slip 2 stitches on to a cable needle, leave at the front of the work, k.2, knit the 2 stitches on the cable needle*.
Repeat Rows 2-5.

Cable stitch

Cable stitch
Cast on a multiple of 9 stitches, plus 3.
Row 1: *p.3, k.3*, p.3.
Rows 2, 3 and 4: work each stitch as it appears on the needle.
Row 5: *p.3, slip 3 stitches on to a cable needle and leave at the back of the work, k.3, knit the 3 stitches on the cable needle*, p.3.
Row 6: repeat from Row 2.

Alternating cable

Cast on a multiple of 4 stitches, plus 2.

Rows 1 and 3: *k.2, p.2,* k.2.

Rows 2 and 4: p.2, *k.2, p.2*.

Row 5: *cross 2 stitches knitwise to slant left (passing behind the first stitch on the left-hand needle, knit the second stitch and then knit the first), p.2*, cross 2 stitches knitwise to slant left.

Rows 6, 8 and 10: work the stitches as they appear on the needle.

Simple cable

Alternating cable

Rows 7 and 9: *p.2, k.2*, p.2.

Row 11: *p.2, cross 2 knitwise to slant left*, p.2.

Row 12: repeat from row 2.

Link cable

Simple cable

Cast on a multiple of 7 stitches, plus 3.

Row 1: *p.3, k.4*, p.3.

Rows 2, 3 and 4: work each stitch as it appears on the needle.

Row 5: *p.3, slip next 2 stitches on to a cable needle and leave at front of work, k.2, k.2 from cable needle*, p.3.

Rows 6, 8 and 10: as Row 2.

Rows 7 and 9: as Row 1.

Row 11: repeat from Row 5.

Link cable

Cast on a multiple of 11 stitches, plus 3.

Row 1: *p.3, k.8*, p.3.

Rows 2, 3 and 4: work each stitch as it appears on the needle.

Row 5: *p.3, slip next 2 stitches on to a cable needle and leave at back of work, k.2, k.2 from cable needle, slip next 2 stitches on to a cable needle and leave at

front of work, k.2, k.2 from cable needle*, p.3.
Rows 6-10: work each stitch as it appears on the needle.
Row 11: as Row 5.
Row 12: repeat from Row 1.

Double cable
Cast on a multiple of 23 stitches, plus 5.
Row 1: *p.5, k.18*, p.5.
Row 2 and even rows: work each stitch as it appears on the needle.
Row 3: *p.5, (slip next 3 stitches on to a cable needle and leave at back of work, k.3, k.3 from cable needle) 3 times*, p.5.
Row 5: as Row 1.
Row 7: *p.5, k.3, (slip next 3 stitches on to a cable needle and leave at front of work, k.3, k.3 from cable needle) twice, k.3*, p.5.
Row 9: repeat from Row 1.

Seed stitch diamond pattern

Double cable

Seed stitch diamond pattern
Cast on a multiple of 14 stitches.
Row 1: *(p.1, k.1) 4 times, k.6*.
Row 2 and even rows: work each stitch as it appears on the needle.
Row 3: *(k.1, p.1) 3 times, k.4, p.1, k.3*.
Row 5: *k.2, p.1, k.1, p.1, k.4, p.1, k.1, p.1, k.2*.
Row 7: *k.3, p.1, k.4, (p.1, k.1) 3 times*.
Row 9: *k.6, (k.1, p.1) 4 times*.
Row 11: as Row 7.
Row 13: as Row 5.
Row 15: as Row 3.
Row 17: repeat from Row 1.

Stockinette stitch diamond pattern
Cast on a multiple of 8 stitches.

Stockinette stitch diamond pattern

Row 1: *p.1, k.6, p.1*.
Row 2 and even rows: work each stitch as it appears on the needle.
Row 3: *k.1, p.1, k.4, p.1, k.1*.
Row 5: *(k.2, p.1) twice, k.2*.
Rows 7 and 9: *k.3, p.2, k.3*.
Row 11: as Row 5.
Row 13: as Row 3.
Row 15: as Row 1.
Row 17: repeat from Row 1.

Transverse line pattern

Transverse line pattern
Cast on a multiple of 8 stitches.
Row 1: *p.2, k.6*.
Row 2 and even rows: work each stitch as it appears on the needle.
Row 3: k.2, *p.2, k.6*, p.2, k.4.
Row 5: k.4, *p.2, k.6*, p.2, k.2.
Row 7: *k.6, p.2*.
Row 9: repeat from Row 1.

Ladder of life pattern

Ladder of life pattern
Cast on a multiple of 10 stitches.
Row 1: *k.4, p.6*.
Row 2 and even rows: purl.
Row 3: knit.
Row 5: *p.5, k.4, p.1*.
Row 7: knit.
Row 9: repeat from Row 1.

Fishbone pattern

Fishbone pattern

Cast on a multiple of 28 stitches.

Row 1: *k.6, cross 2 stitches knitwise to slant right (passing in front of the first stitch on the left-hand needle, knit the second stitch and then knit the first), cross 2 stitches knitwise to slant left (passing behind the first stitch on the left-hand needle, knit the second stitch and then knit the first), k.6, cross 2 stitches knitwise to slant left, k.8, cross 2 stitches knitwise to slant right*.

Row 2 and even rows: purl.

Row 3: *k.5, cross 2 stitches knitwise to slant right, k.2, cross 2 stitches knitwise to slant left, k.6, cross 2 stitches knitwise to slant left, k.6, cross 2 stitches knitwise to slant right, k.1*.

Row 5: *k.4, cross 2 right, k.4, cross 2 left, k.6, cross 2 left, k.4, cross 2 right, k.2*.

Row 7: *k.3, cross 2 right, k.6, cross 2 left, k.6, cross 2 left, k.2, cross 2 right, k.3*.

Row 9: *k.2, cross 2 right, k.8, cross 2 left, k.6, cross 2 left, cross 2 right, k.4*.

Row 11: repeat from Row 1.

Large lattice pattern

Cast on a multiple of 16 stitches.

Row 1: *cross 2 stitches knitwise to slant left (see p. 37 and Fishbone pattern above), k.12, cross 2 stitches knitwise to slant right.

Row 2 and even rows: purl.

Row 3: *k.1, cross 2 stitches knitwise to slant left, k.10, cross 2 right, k.1*.

Row 5: *k.2, cross 2 left, k.8, cross 2 right, k.2*.

Row 7: *k.3, cross 2 left, k.6, cross 2 right, k.3*.

Row 9: *k.4, cross 2 left, k.4, cross 2 right, k.4*.

Row 11: *k.5, cross 2 left, k.2, cross 2 right, k.5*.

Row 13: *k.6, cross 2 left, cross 2 right k.6*.

Row 15: *k.6, cross 2 right, cross 2 left, k.6*.

Row 17: *k.5, cross 2 right, k.2, cross 2 left, k.5*.

Row 19: *k.4, cross 2 right, k.4, cross 2 left, k.4*.

Row 21: *k.3, cross 2 right, k.6, cross 2 left, k.3*.

Row 23: *k.2, cross 2 right, k.8, cross 2 left, k.2*.

Row 25: *k.1, cross 2 right, k.10, cross 2 left, k.1*.

Row 27: *cross 2 right, k.12, cross 2 left*.

Row 29: repeat from Row 1.

Large lattice pattern

Trinity stitch

Cast on a multiple of 6 stitches, plus 2.

Row 1: p.2, *knit 4 times into next stitch (knitting alternately into the front and the back), p.2, k.1, p.2*.

Row 2: *k.2, p.1, k.2, k.4 winding the yarn twice around needle for each stitch*, k.2.

Row 3: p.2, *k.4 dropping the extra stitches made in previous row, p.2, k.1, p.2*.

Row 4: as Row 2.

Row 5: as Row 3.

Row 6: *k.2, p.1, k.2, p.4 together*, k.2.

Row 7: p.2, *k.1, p.2, k.4 together, p.2*.

Floral pattern

A crochet hook is required to work this pattern.

Cast on a multiple of 10 stitches.

Row 1: *p.5, yarn to back of work, slip 1 purlwise, yarn forward, p.4*.

Row 2: *k.4, yarn forward, slip 1 purlwise, yarn back, k.5*.

Row 3: as Row 1.

Row 4: as Row 2.

Row 5: *p.3, k.5, p.2*.

Row 6: *k.2, p.5, k.3*.

Row 7: *p.3 **using a crochet hook, take the right-hand thread of the stitch slipped in Row 4, put yarn around crochet hook, make a loop, yarn around hook and make a second loop, pull one loop through the other and transfer the stitch thus obtained to the right-hand needle**, k.5, repeat from ** to ** taking the left-hand thread of the same slipped stitch, p.2*.

Row 8: *k.2, p.2 together, p.3, p.2 together, k.3*.

Row 9: *p.5, k.1, p.4*.

Row 10: knit.

Row 11: *yarn back, slip 1 purlwise, p.9*.

Row 12: *k.9, yarn forward, slip 1 purlwise*.

Row 13: as Row 11.

Row 14: as Row 12.

Row 15: *k.3, p.5, k.2*.

Trinity stitch

Row 8: *k.2, k.4 winding yarn twice around needle for each stitch, k.2, p.1*, k.2.

Row 9: p.2, *k.1, p.2, k.4 dropping the extra stitches made in previous row, p.2*.

Row 10: as Row 8.

Row 11: as Row 9.

Row 12: *k.2, p.4 together, k.2, p.1*, k.2.

Row 13: repeat from Row 1.

Floral pattern

Row 16: *p.2, k.5, p.3*.
Row 17: k.3, using the crochet hook take the left-hand thread of the stitch slipped in Row 14 and make loops as in Row 7, *p.5, using the crochet hook take the right-hand thread of the second flower and make loops, k.5, take the left-hand thread of the same flower and make loops*, k.2.
Row 18: p.2, *k.5, p.2 together, p.3, p.2 together*, p.3.
Row 19: *k.1, p.9*.
Row 20: knit.
Row 21: repeat from Row 1.

Window pattern
Cast on a multiple of 12 stitches.
Row 1: *k.6, (p.2, transfer these 2 stitches to the left-hand needle, yarn back, transfer the 2 stitches back to the right-hand needle) 3 times*.
Row 2 and even rows: purl.
Row 3: as Row 1.
Row 5: as Row 1.
Row 7: *(p.2, transfer these 2 stitches to the left-hand needle, yarn back, transfer the 2 stitches back to the right-hand needle) 3 times, k.6*.
Row 9: as Row 7.
Row 11: as Row 7.
Row 13: repeat from Row 1.

Window pattern

Flower pattern

Flower pattern
Cast on a multiple of 8 stitches, plus 3.
Row 1: knit.
Row 2 and even rows: purl.
Row 3: knit.
Row 5: *k.5, p.3 together and do not slip stitches off the left-hand needle, knit the same 3 together, then purl the same 3 together; slip stitches on to the right-hand needle*, k.3.
Row 7: knit.
Row 9: knit.
Row 11: knit.

Row 13: *p.3 together and do not slip stitches off the left-hand needle, knit same 3 together, then purl the same 3 together, k.5, p.3 together and do not slip off left-hand needle, knit same 3 together, then purl same 3 together and slip on to the right-hand needle*.
Row 15: repeat from Row 3.

Leaf pattern 1

Cast on a multiple of 24 stitches, plus 2.

Row 1: *p.2, k.6, k.3 together, yarn around needle (see p. 34), k.1, yarn around needle, p.2, yarn around needle, k.1, yarn around needle, k.3 together through back of loop, k.6*, p.2.

Row 2 and even rows: *k.2, p.10*, k.2.

Row 3: *p.2, k.4, k.3 together, k.1, yarn around needle, k.1, yarn around needle, k.1, p.2, k.1, yarn around needle, k.1, yarn around needle, k.1, k.3 together through back of loop, k.4*, p.2.

Row 5: *p.2, k.2, k.3 together, k.2, yarn around needle, k.1, yarn around needle, k.2, p.2, k.2, yarn around needle, k.1, yarn around needle, k.2, k.3 together through back of loop, k.2*, p.2.

Row 7: *p.2, k.3 together, k.3, yarn around needle, k.1, yarn around needle, k.3, p.2, k.3, yarn around needle, k.1, yarn

Leaf pattern 2

Cast on a multiple of 12 stitches, plus 6, plus edge stitches.

Row 1:*k.1, yarn around needle, slip 1, k.1, pass slip stitch over, k.7, k.2 together, yarn around needle*, k.1, yarn around needle, slip 1, k.1, pass slip stitch over, k.3.

Row 2 and even rows: purl.

Row 3: *k.1, yarn around needle, k.1, slip 1, k.1, pass slip stitch over, k.5, k.2 together, k.1, yarn around needle*, k.1, yarn around needle, k.1, slip 1, k.1, pass slip stitch over, k.2.

Row 5: *k.1, yarn around needle, k.2, slip 1, k.1, pass slip stitch over, k.3, k.2 together, k.2, yarn around needle, * k.1, yarn around needle, k.2, slip 1, k.1, pass slip stitch over, k.1.

Row 7: *k.1, yarn around needle, k.3, slip 1, k.1, pass slip stitch over, k.1, k.2 together, k.3, yarn around needle*, k.1, yarn around needle, k.3, slip 1, k.1, pass slip stitch over.

Row 9: *k.1, yarn around needle, k.4, slip 1, k.2 together, pass slip stitch over, k.4, yarn around needle*, k.1, yarn around needle, k.5.

Row 11: *k.4, k.2 together, yarn around needle, k.1, yarn around needle, slip 1, k.1, pass slip stitch over, k.3*, k.4, k.2

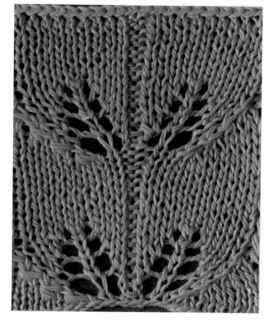

Leaf pattern 1

around needle, k.3, k.3 together through back of loop*, p.2.

Rows 9, 11 and 13: *p.2, k.10 *, p.2.

Row 17: repeat from Row 1.

Leaf pattern 2

together, yarn around needle, k.1.

Row 13: *k.3, k.2 together, k.1, yarn around needle, k.1, yarn around needle, k.1, slip 1, k.1, pass slip stitch over, k.2*, k.3, k.2 together, k.1, yarn around needle, k.1.

Row 15: *k.2, k.2 together, k.2, yarn around needle, k.1, yarn around needle, k.2, slip 1, k.1, pass slip stitch over, k.1*, k.1, k.2 together, k.3, yarn around needle, k.1.

Row 17: *k.1, k.2 together, k.3, yarn around needle, k.1, yarn around needle, k.3, slip 1, k.1, pass slip stitch over*, k.1, k.2 together, k.3, yarn around needle, k.1.

Row 19: k.2 together, *k.4, yarn around needle, k.1, yarn around needle, k.4, slip 1, k.2 together, pass slip stitch over*, k.4.

Row 21: repeat from Row 1.

Row 5: k.3, yarn around needle, *k.1, slip 1, k.2 together, pass slip stitch over, k.1, yarn around needle, k.5, yarn around needle*, k.1, slip 1, k.1, pass slip stitch over.

Row 7: k.4, yarn around needle *slip 1, k.2 together, pass slip stitch over, yarn around needle, k.7, yarn around needle*, slip 1, k.1, pass slip stitch over.

Row 9: slip 1, k.1, pass slip stitch over, k.3, yarn around needle, *k.1, yarn around needle, k.3, slip 1, k.2 together, pass slip stitch over, k.3, yarn around needle*, k.1.

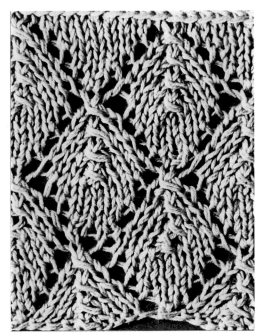

Leaf pattern 3

Leaf pattern 3

Cast on a multiple of 10 stitches, plus 6.

Row 1: k.1, yarn around needle, *k.3, slip 1, k.2 together, pass slip stitch over, k.3, yarn around needle, k.1, yarn around needle*, k.3, slip 1, k.1, pass slip stitch over.

Row 2 and even rows: purl.

Row 3: k.2, yarn around needle, *k.2, slip 1, k.2 together, pass slip stitch over, k.2, yarn around needle, k.3, yarn around needle*, k.2, slip 1, k.1, pass slip stitch over.

Row 11: slip 1, k.1, pass slip stitch over, k.2, yarn around needle, k.1, *k.2, yarn around needle, k.2, slip 1, k.2 together, pass slip stitch over, k.1, yarn around needle, k.2*, k.1.

Row 13: slip 1, k.1, pass slip stitch over, k.1, yarn around needle, k.2, *k.3, yarn around needle, k.1, slip 1, k.2 together, pass slip stitch over, k.1, yarn around needle, k.2*, k.1.

Row 15: slip 1, k.1, pass slip stitch over, yarn around needle, k.3, *k.4, yarn around needle, slip 1, k.2 together, pass slip stitch over, yarn around needle, k.3*, k.1.

Row 17: repeat from Row 1.

Diamond eyelet pattern

Cast on a multiple of 16 stitches, plus edge stitches.

Row 1: *k.6, k.2 together, yarn around needle, k.1, yarn around needle, k.2 together, k.5*.

Row 2 and even rows: knit.

Row 3: *k.5, k.2 together, yarn around needle, k.3, yarn around needle, k.2 together, k.4*.

Row 5: *k.4, k.2 together, yarn around needle, k.5, yarn around needle, k.2 together, k.3*.

Row 7: *k.3, k.2 together, yarn around needle, k.7, yarn around needle, k.2 together, k.2*.

Row 9: *k.2, k.2 together, yarn around needle, k.9, yarn around needle, k.2

together, k.3, k.2 together, yarn around needle, k.4*.

Row 21: *k.6, yarn around needle, k.2 together, k.1, k.2 together, yarn around needle, k.5*.

Row 23: repeat from Row 1.

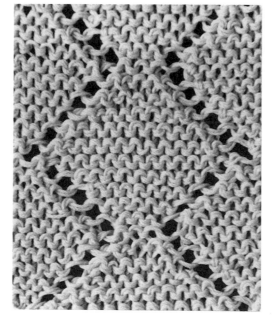

Diamond eyelet pattern

together, k.1*.

Row 11: *k.1, k.2 together, yarn around needle, k.11, yarn around needle, k.2 together, k.2*.

Row 13: *k.2, yarn around needle, k.2 together, k.9, k.2 together, yarn around needle, k.2*.

Row 15: *k.3, yarn around needle, k.2 together, k.7, k.2 together, yarn around needle, k.2*.

Row 17: *k.4, yarn around needle, k.2 together, k.5, k.2 together, yarn around needle, k.3*.

Row 19: *k.5, yarn around needle, k.2

Fagotting stitch 1

Cast on an even number of stitches, plus edge stitches.

Work every row as follows: *yarn around needle, p.2 together*.

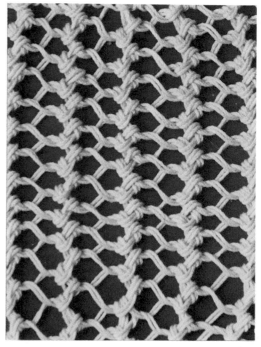

Fagotting stitch 1

Fagotting stitch 2

Cast on an even number of stitches, plus edge stitches.

Work every row as follows: *yarn around needle, slip 1, k.1, pass slip stitch over*.

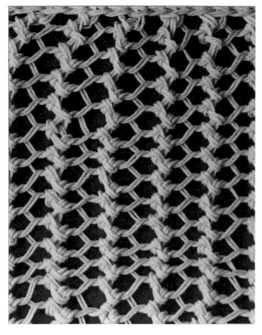

Fagotting stitch 2

Vertical openwork stitch 2

Cast on a multiple of 4 stitches.

Row 1: *k.2, yarn around needle, slip 1, k.1, pass slip stitch over*.

Row 2: *p.2, yarn around needle, p.2 together*.

Row 3: repeat from Row 1.

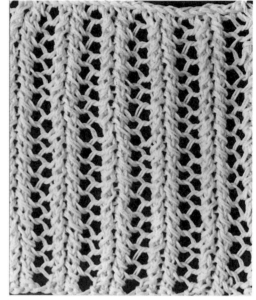

Vertical openwork stitch 2

Vertical openwork stitch 1

Cast on a multiple of 6 stitches, plus 3.

Row 1: *p.3, yarn around needle, slip 1

Lace stitch

Cast on a multiple of 4 stitches.

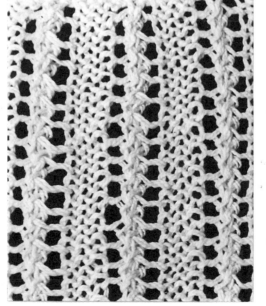

Vertical openwork stitch 1

purlwise, p.2 together, pass slip stitch over, yarn around needle*, p.3.

Row 2: k.3, *p.3, k.3*.

Row 3: repeat from Row 1.

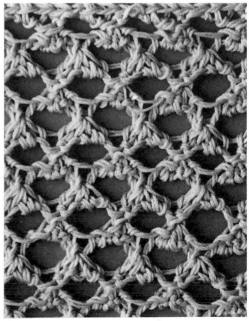

Lace stitch

Row 1: p.2, *yarn around needle, p.4 together*, p.2.
Row 2: k.2, *k.1, (k.1, p.1, k.1) into the yarn around needle of the previous row.
Row 3: knit.
Row 4: repeat from Row 1.

Ace of spades stitch

Cast on a multiple of 7 stitches, plus edge stitches.
Row 1: *k.2, k.2 together, yarn around needle, k.3*.
Row 2: *p.1, p.2 together through back of loop, yarn around needle, p.1, yarn around needle, p.2 together, p.1*.
Row 3: *k.2 together, yarn around needle, k.3, yarn around needle, slip 1, k.1, pass slip stitch over*.
Row 4: purl.
Row 5: *yarn around needle, slip 1, k.1, pass slip stitch over, k.5*.
Row 6: *yarn around needle, p.2 together,

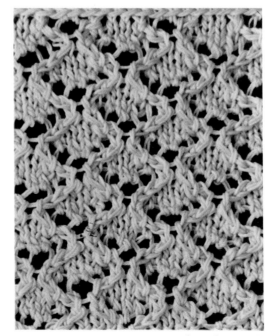

Ace of spades stitch

p.2, p.2 together through back of loop, yarn around needle, p.1*.
Row 7: *k.2, yarn around needle, slip 1, k.1, pass slip stitch over, k.2 together, yarn around needle, k.1*.
Row 8: purl.
Row 9: repeat from Row 1.

Vertical zig-zag stitch

Cast on a multiple of 3 stitches, plus 3.
Row 1: k.1, *yarn around needle, k.2 together through back of loop, k.1*, k.2.
Row 2 and even rows: purl.
Row 3: k.2, *yarn around needle, k.2 together through back of loop, k.1*, k.1.
Row 5: k.3, *yarn around needle, k.2 together through back of loop, k.1*.
Row 7: k.1, *k.2 together through back of loop, yarn around needle, k.1*, k.2.
Row 9: *k.2 together, yarn around needle, k.1*, k.3.

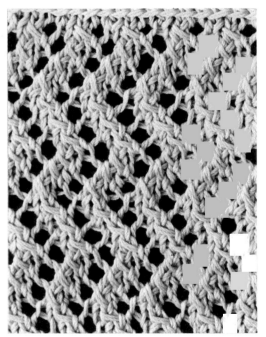

Vertical zig-zag pattern

Row 11: k.1, *yarn around needle, k.1, k.2 together*, k.2.
Row 13: k.2 together, yarn around needle, *yarn around needle, k.2 together through back of loop, k.1*, k.1.
Row 15: k.3, *yarn around needle, k.2 together through back of loop, k.1*.
Row 17: k.1, *k.2 together through back of loop, k.1, yarn around needle*, k.2.
Row 19: repeat from Row 7.

Horizontal zig-zag pattern

Cast on a multiple of 8 stitches, plus 1, plus edge stitches.

Row 1: *k.5, yarn around needle, k.2 together, k.1*, k.1.

Row 2 and even rows: purl.

Row 3: *k.3, k.2 together through back of loop, yarn around needle, k.1, yarn around needle, k.2 together*, k.1.

Row 5: k.1, *k.1, k.2 together through back of loop, yarn around needle, k.3, yarn around needle, k.2 together*.

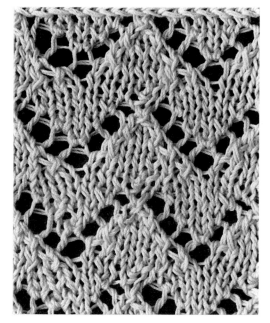

Horizontal zig-zag pattern

Row 7: *yarn around needle, k.2 together through back of loop, transfer stitch just knitted to left-hand needle and pass next stitch over, transfer stitch to right-hand needle, yarn around needle, k.5*, k.1.

Row 9: *k.1, knit into the front and back of next stitch, k.6*, k.1.

Row 11: k.2 together, k.4, yarn around needle, k.2 together, *k.2 together, k.5, yarn around needle, k.2 together*, k.2.

Row 13: repeat from Row 3.

Horseshoe pattern

Cast on a multiple of 10 stitches, plus edge stitches.

Row 1: *yarn around needle, k.3, slip 1, k.2 together, pass slip stitch over, k.3, yarn around needle, k.1*.

Row 2 and even rows: purl.

Row 3: *k.1, yarn around needle, k.2, slip 1, k.2 together, pass slip stitch over, k.2, yarn around needle, k.2*.

Row 5: *k.2, yarn around needle, k.1, slip 1, k.2 together, pass slip stitch over, k.1, yarn around needle, k.3*.

Row 7: *k.3, yarn around needle, slip 1, k.2 together, pass slip stitch over, yarn around needle, k.4*.

Row 9: repeat from Row 1.

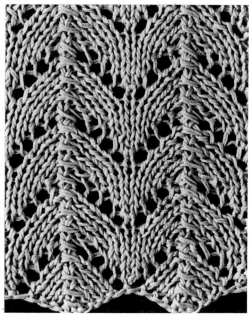

Horseshoe pattern

Eyelet honeycomb pattern

Cast on a multiple of 8 stitches, plus 6.
Row 1: purl.
Row 2: knit.
Row 3: purl.
Row 4: p.5, *p.1, keep yarn at front, slip 2 purlwise, p.5*, p.1.
Row 5: k.1, *k.5, keep yarn at back, slip 2 purlwise, k.1*, k.5.
Row 6: p.5, *p.1, keep yarn at front, slip 2 purlwise, p.5*, p.1.
Row 7: k.1, *slip 1, k.1, pass slip stitch over, yarn around needle, k.2 together, k.1, keep yarn at back, slip 2 purlwise, k.1*, slip 1, k.1, pass slip stitch over, yarn

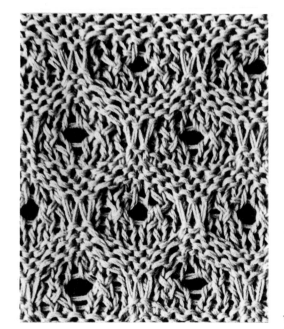

Eyelet honeycomb pattern

around needle, k.2 together, k.1.
Row 8: p.1, purl into the front and back of the yarn around needle stitch of the previous row, p.1,* p.1, yarn forward, slip 2 purlwise, p.2, p.2 into the yarn around needle stitch of the previous row, p.1*, p.1.
Row 9: k.1, *k.5, yarn back, slip 2 purlwise, k.1*, k.5.
Row 10: knit.
Row 11: purl.
Row 12: knit.
Row 13: k.1, *k.1, yarn back, slip 2 purlwise, k.5*, k.1, yarn back, slip 2 purlwise, k.2.
Row 14: p.2, yarn forward, slip 2 purlwise, p.1, *p.5, yarn forward, slip 2 purlwise, p.1*, p.1.
Row 15: k.1, *k.1, yarn back, slip 2 purlwise, k.5*, k.1, yarn back, slip 2 purlwise, k.2.
Row 16: p.2, yarn forward, slip 2 purlwise, p.1, *p.2 together, yarn around needle, p.1, replace stitch on left-hand needle, pass next stitch over with tip of right-hand needle from left to right, replace stitch on right-hand needle, p.1, yarn forward, slip 2 purlwise, p.1*, p.1.
Row 17: k.1, *k.1, yarn back, slip 2 purlwise, k.2, knit into the front and back of the yarn forward stitch of the previous row, k.1*, k.1, yarn back, p.2, k.2.
Row 18: p.2, yarn forward, slip 2 purlwise, p.1, *p.5, yarn forward, slip 2 purlwise, p.1*, p.1.
Row 19: repeat from Row 1.

Wing pattern

Cast on a multiple of 8 stitches, plus edge stitches.

Row 1: *p.7, k.1, yarn around needle*.
Row 2: *p.2, k.7*.
Row 3: *p.7, k.2, yarn around needle*.
Row 4: *p.3, k.7*.
Row 5: *p.7, k.3, yarn around needle*.

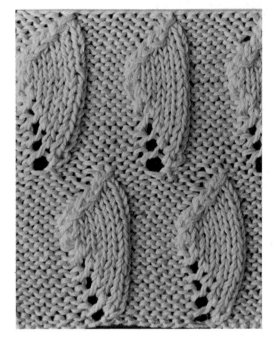

Wing pattern

Row 6: *p.4, k.7*.
Row 7: *p.7, k.4, yarn around needle*.
Row 8: *p.5, k.7*.
Row 9: *p.7, k.5, yarn around needle*.
Row 10: *p.6, k.7*.
Row 11: *p.7, k.6, yarn around needle*.
Row 12: *p.7, k.7*.
Row 13: *p.7, k.5, k.2 together*.
Row 14: *p.2 together, p.4, k.7*.
Row 15: *p.7, k.3, k.2 together*.
Row 16: *p.2 together, p.2, k.7*.
Row 17: *p.7, k.1, k.2 together*.
Row 18: *p.2 together, k.7*.
Row 19: *p.3, k.1, yarn around needle, p.4*.
Row 20: *k.4, p.2, k.3*.
Row 21: *p.3, k.2, yarn around needle, p.4*.
Row 22: *k.4, p.3, k.3*.
Row 23: *p.3, k.3, yarn around needle, p.4*.
Row 24: *k.4, p.4, k.3*.
Row 25: *p.3, k.4, yarn around needle, p.4*.
Row 26: *k.4, p.5, k.3*.
Row 27: *p.3, k.5, yarn around needle, p.4*.
Row 28: *k.4, p.6, k.3*.
Row 29: *p.3, k.6, yarn around needle, p.4*.
Row 30: *k.4, p.7, k.3*.
Row 31: *p.3, k.5, k.2 together, p.4*.
Row 32: *k.4, p.2 together, p.4, k.3*.
Row 33: *p.3, k.3, k.2 together, p.4*.
Row 34: *k.4, p.2 together, p.4*.
Row 35: *p.3, k.1, k.2 together, p.4*.
Row 36: *k.4, p.2 together, k.3*.
Row 37: repeat from Row 1.

Butterfly pattern

Cast on a multiple of 10 stitches.

Row 1: *k.2 together, yarn around needle, k.1, yarn around needle, slip 1, k.1, pass slip stitch over, k.5*.
Row 2: *p.7, slip 1 purlwise, p.2*.
Row 3: as Row 1.
Row 4: as Row 2.
Row 5: knit.
Row 6: purl.
Row 7: *k.5, k.2 together, yarn around needle, k.1, yarn around needle, slip 1, k.1, pass slip stitch over*.
Row 8: *p.2, slip 1 purlwise, p.7*.
Row 9: as Row 7.
Row 10: as Row 8.
Row 11: as Row 5.
Row 12: as Row 6.
Row 13: repeat from Row 1.

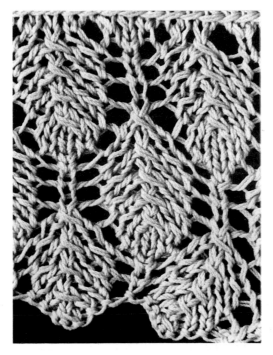

Row 2 and even rows: purl.
Row 3: k.2, *yarn around needle, k.2, slip 1, k.2 together, pass slip stitch over, k.2, yarn around needle, k.1*, k.1.
Row 5: k.2, *yarn around needle, k.2, slip 1, k.2 together, pass slip stitch over, k.2, yarn around needle, k.1*, k.1.
Row 7: k.2, *k.1, yarn around needle, k.1, slip 1, k.2 together, pass slip stitch over, k.1, yarn around needle, k.2*, k.1.
Row 9: k.2, *k.2, yarn around needle, k.1, slip 1, k.1, pass slip stitch over, yarn around needle, k.3*, k.1.
Row 11: k.1, k.2 together, *k.2, yarn around needle, k.1, yarn around needle, k.2, slip 1, k.2 together, pass slip stitch over*, yarn around needle.
Row 13: k.1, k.2 together, *k.2, yarn around needle, k.1, yarn around needle, k.2, slip 1, k.2 together, pass slip stitch over*, yarn around needle.
Row 15: k.1, k.2 together, *k.2, yarn around needle, k.1, yarn around needle, k.2, slip 1, k.2 together, pass slip stitch over*, yarn around needle.
Row 17: k.1, k.2 together, *k.1, yarn around needle, k.3, yarn around needle, k.1, slip 1, k.2 together, pass slip stitch over*, yarn around needle.
Row 19: k.1, k.2 together, *yarn around needle, k.5, yarn around needle, slip 1, k.2 together, pass slip stitch over*.
Row 21: repeat from Row 1.

Butterfly pattern

Pine cone pattern
Cast on a multiple of 8 stitches, plus 3, plus edge stitches.
Row 1: k.2, *yarn around needle, k.2, slip 1, k.2 together, pass slip stitch over, k.2, yarn around needle, k.1*, k.1.

Pine cone pattern

Eyelet cable pattern
Cast on a multiple of 16 stitches.
Row 1: *k.3, k.2 together, k.2, yarn around needle, k.5, yarn around needle, k.2, slip 1, k.1, pass slip stitch over*.
Row 2 and even rows: purl.
Row 3: *k.2, k.2 together, k.2, yarn around needle, k.1, yarn around needle, k.2, slip 1, k.1, pass slip stitch over, k.5*.
Row 5: *k.1, k.2 together, k.2, yarn around needle, k.3, yarn around needle, k.2, slip 1, k.1, pass slip stitch over, k.4*.
Row 7: *k.2 together, k.2, yarn around needle, k.5, yarn around needle, k.2, slip 1, k.1, pass slip stitch over, k.3*.
Row 9: *k.5, k.2 together, k.2, yarn around needle, k.1, yarn around needle,

k.2, slip 1, k.1, pass slip stitch over, k.2*.
Row 11: *k.4, k.2 together, k.2, yarn around needle, k.3, yarn around needle, k.2, slip 1, k.1, pass slip stitch over, k.1*.
Row 13: repeat from Row 1.

Row 3: *yarn around needle, k.4, yarn around needle*.
Row 4: *p.1, p.2 together twice, k.1*.
Row 5: repeat from Row 1.

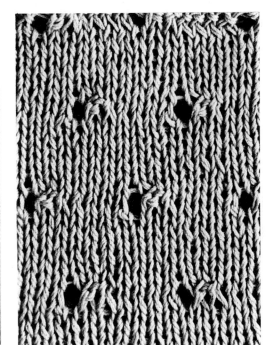

Simple eyelet pattern

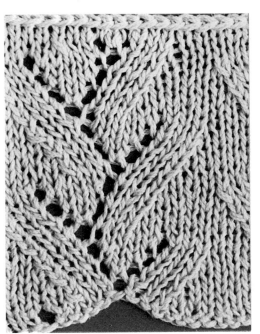

Eyelet cable pattern

Simple eyelet pattern
Cast on a multiple of 7 stitches, plus 1.
Row 1: *k.5, yarn around needle, p.2 together*, k.1.
Rows 2-8: work in stockinette stitch.
Row 9: k.1, *yarn around needle, p.2 together, k.5*.
Rows 10-16: work in stockinette stitch.
Row 17: repeat from Row 1.

Openwork stitch

Openwork stitch
Cast on a multiple of 4 stitches, plus edge stitches.
Row 1. *k.2, yarn around needle twice, k.2*.
Row 2: *p.2 together, k.1, p.1, p.2 together*.

Diagonal openwork stitch

Cast on a multiple of 5 stitches.

Row 1 and odd rows: knit.

Row 2: *p.3, yarn around needle, p.2 together*.

Row 4: p.4, *yarn around needle, p.2 together, p.3*, p.1.

Row 6: p.5, *yarn around needle, p.2 tog, p.3*.

Row 8: p.1, *yarn around needle, p.2 together, p.3*, yarn around needle, p.2 together, p.2.

Row 10: p.2, *yarn around needle, p.2 together, p.3*, yarn around needle, p.2 together, p.1.

Row 12: repeat from Row 2.

k.3, make a third loop in the same stitch, k.5*.

Row 6: *p.5, purl the third loop of the previous row with the next stitch, p.1, purl the second loop of the previous row with the next stitch, p.1, purl the first loop of the previous row with the next stitch*.

Row 7: knit.

Row 8: purl.

Row 9: knit.

Row 10: purl.

Row 11: *k.5, insert the right-hand needle into the eighth stitch of the eighth row, yarn around needle, make a loop, k.2, make a second loop in the same stitch, k.3, make a third loop in the same stitch*.

Row 12: *purl the third loop of the previous row with the next stitch, p.1, purl the second loop of the previous row with the next stitch, p.1, purl the first loop of the previous row with the next stitch, p.5*.

Diagonal openwork pattern

Bouquet pattern

Bouquet pattern

Cast on a multiple of 10 stitches.

Row 1: knit.

Row 2: purl.

Row 3: knit.

Row 4: purl.

Row 5: *insert the right-hand needle into the third stitch of the first row, yarn around needle, draw yarn through, k.2, make a second loop in the same stitch,

Row 13: knit.

Row 14: purl.

Row 15: repeat from Row 5.

Forty-two garments for you to make

The following pages offer a choice of designs for men, women and children. The patterns have been graded according to the degree of expertise required, from one to three stars (★ = beginner, ★★ = intermediate, ★★★ = advanced).

Instructions for one or more alternative sizes are given in brackets after the first size. We recommend that the knitter underline in pencil the relevant size throughout the pattern before beginning work. Sizes for adult garments are based on chest measurements.

Both continental and American needle sizes are given.

The stitches employed are, with one or two exceptions, those most frequently in use: nothing need prevent you however from using different stitches if you prefer, but remember to modify the tension and other measurements if you do so.

The patterns

Jacquard cap (1)
Illustrated in colour on p. 85

Standard: ★★★
Tension: 16 stitches and 20 rows to 10cm(4")
Size: To fit children aged 8-13
Materials: 40g(2oz) natural wool in dark brown
20g(1oz) natural wool in light brown
20g(1oz) natural wool in white
1 pair needles size 4mm(#6)
Stitches used: Jacquard knitting (see pp. 52-3). Single rib (see p. 57). Stockinette stitch (see p. 57).

Method
● With dark brown wool cast on 75 stitches using one of the invisible methods of casting on described on pp. 30-1. Work 3 rows in k.1, slip 1 rib (see p. 30). Continue in stockinette stitch and Jacquard, changing colours as shown on the first chart. Work through this chart once.

Work 4 rows in k.1, p.1 rib using dark brown wool. The wrong side of the work is now facing; work 3 rows in stockinette stitch in dark brown. Continue in stockinette stitch and Jacquard, repeating the first chart once.

Work 2 rows in stockinette stitch and dark brown wool. Continuing in stockinette stitch and Jacquard, work the second chart. With dark brown wool work 2 rows in stockinette stitch. Change to the light brown wool and work 2 more rows, decreasing 1 stitch every 5 stitches on both rows.

Continue in stockinette stitch with dark brown wool, decreasing on every row as above until 6 stitches remain. Draw the wool through these stitches and fasten off.
● *To make up:* Join the border on the wrong side. Join sides of the rest of the cap also on the wrong side. Fold back border.

Colour chart for the two border stripes
□ Dark brown background
○ White
◇ Light brown

Colour chart for the cap
□ White background
○ Light brown
◇ Dark brown

Flecked scarf (2)
Illustrated in colour on p. 85

Standard: ★
Tension: 16 stitches and 15 rows to 10cm(4")
Materials: 240g(9oz) flecked green and beige wool, 3-ply
1 pair needles size 6mm(#10)
1 crochet hook size 6mm (#1)
Stitches used: Double rib (see p. 58).

The garments illustrated in colour on p. 85.

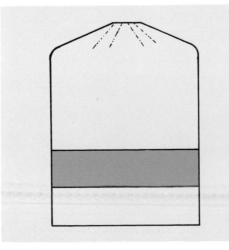

Method

- Using wool double cast on 40 stitches and work in double rib for 100cm(40″).
- *To make up:* Using 4 strands of wool together make a fringe (see p. 137), 13cm(5″) in length, at each end of the scarf.

Jacquard cardigan (3)

Illustrated in colour on p. 85

Standard: ★★★

Tension: 16 stitches and 20 rows to 10cm(4″)

Size: To fit children aged 10-11. The figures in brackets refer to sizes for 8-9 and 12-13 years.

Materials: 350g(300g–400g)/12oz(11oz–14oz) natural wool in dark brown

150g(100g–200g)/5½oz(4oz–7oz) natural wool in white

80g(50g–100g)/3½oz(2oz–4oz) natural wool in light brown

1 pair needles size 4mm(#6)

6 metal buttons

Stitches used: Single rib (see p. 57). Jacquard knitting (see pp. 52-3).

Method

- *Back:* With dark brown wool cast on 64(60–70) stitches using one of the invisible methods of casting on described on pp. 30-1; work 3 rows in k.1 slip 1 rib. Continue in single rib until work measures 6cm(2½″).

  Continue in stockinette stitch and Jacquard, following the chart, until work measures 43(40–60)cm/17(15½–18)″. Bind off.

- *Fronts:* With dark brown wool cast on 30(26–34) stitches as for back; work 3 rows in k.1 slip 1 rib. Continue in single rib until work measures 6cm(2½″).

  Continue in stockinette stitch and Jacquard, following the chart, until work measures 38(36–40)cm/15(14–16)″.

  With right side facing, bind off for the neck thus: on alternate rows bind off 4 stitches, 2 stitches and 1 stitch. Continue until front measures same as back. Bind off.

  Complete other side to match, reversing shapings.

- *Sleeves:* With dark brown wool cast on 36(34–38) stitches as for back. Work 3

The garments illustrated in colour on p. 85.

Chart for the Jacquard cardigan
□ Dark brown background
◇ Light brown
○ White

rows in k.1 slip 1 rib. Continue in single rib for 12cm(5″).

Continue in stockinette stitch and Jacquard for 30(28–32)cm/12(11–12½)″ following the chart and increasing one stitch at each end of every fourth row. Bind off.

- *To make up:* Join the shoulder and side seams, leaving a gap wide enough for the sleeves. Join sleeve seams and insert sleeves.

  With the crochet hook and the dark brown wool pick up the stitches along the center fronts (see p. 42) and work these stitches in k.1 slip 1 rib for 5cm(2″). Bind off the stitches by the invisible method (see p. 31). When making these borders 6 horizontal buttonholes should be worked (see p. 45) over 2 stitches, 7cm(2½″) apart.

  Still using the dark brown wool, pick up the stitches around the neck, starting from the right front. Work in single rib for

7cm(2½″), then increase 1 stitch at each end of every 2 rows. When collar is desired depth, work 2 rows in k.1 slip 1 rib. Bind off by the invisible method.

Stitch the buttons opposite the buttonholes. Fold the ribbed borders on the sleeves in half.

Flecked socks (4)
Illustrated in colour on p. 85

Standard: ★★★

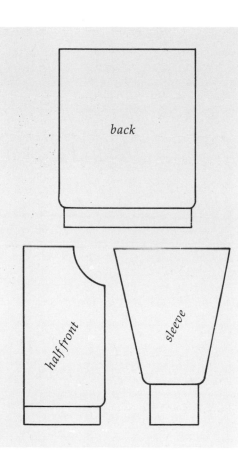

Tension: 26 stitches and 34 rows to 10cm(4″)
Size: To fit children aged 10-11 (shoe size 4½–5). The figures in brackets refer to sizes for 8-9 years (shoe size 2½-4) and 6-7 years (shoe size 1-2½).
Materials: 100g(80g–60g)/4oz(3½oz–2½oz) flecked green and beige wool, 3-ply
1 set of 4 needles size 2.5mm(#1)
1 set of 4 needles size 3mm(#3)

Stitches used: Single rib (see p. 57). Stockinette stitch (see p. 57). Double rib (see p. 58).

Method
• With the set of 4 needles size 2.5mm(#1) cast on 44(40–36) stitches using one of the invisible methods of casting on described on pp. 30-1. Work 5 rows in k.1 slip 1 rib. Change to the size 3mm(#3) set of needles and continue in double rib for 28(40–36)cm/11(9½–8½)″. Start to shape the heel, working the 14(12–10) stitches in the center in stockinette stitch. Using one of the methods described on pp. 133-4 continue to work the sole of the foot in stockinette stitch. When it measures 17(15–13)cm/6½(6–5½)″, begin to decrease for the toe using one of the methods described on p. 134.
• *To make up:* Close the toe using tiny stitches on the wrong side. Finish off. Thread elastic through the k.1 slip 1 rib at the top.

Blue angora slipover (5)
Illustrated in colour on p. 85

Standard: ★★
Tension: 26 stitches and 32 rows to 10cm(4″)
Size: To fit children aged 12-13. The figures in brackets refer to sizes for 10-11 and 8-9 years.
Materials: 100g(80g–60g)/4oz(3½oz–2½oz) blue Angora
10g(½oz) white Angora
1 pair needles size 2.5mm(#1)
1 pair needles size 3mm(#3)
Stitches used: Double rib (see p. 58). Stockinette stitch (see p. 57).

Method
• The slipover is worked in one piece, starting at the back and ending at the lower edge of the front.

With white wool and size 2.5mm(#1) needles cast on 105(98–90) stitches and work in double rib for 4 rows. Change to blue wool and continue working in rib for 3cm(1½″). Change to size 3mm(#3) needles and work in stockinette stitch for 26(23–20)cm/10(9–8)″.

For the armholes, decrease 3 stitches, then 2 stitches, at each end of alternate

The garments illustrated in colour on p. 85.

The garments illustrated in colour on p. 86.

rows. Continue in stockinette stitch for another 16(15–14)cm/6½(6–5½)″.

Bind off the 55(52–48) central stitches and work the remaining 20(18–16) stitches on either side for the shoulder separately. Work 2cm(1″) on each side. Cast on the central stitches again and continue on all the stitches for 16(15–14)cm/6½(6–5¼)″.

For the armholes cast on 2 stitches,

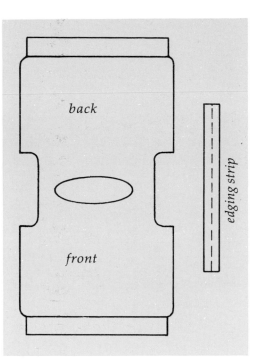

then 3 stitches, at each end of alternate rows. Continue in stockinette stitch until the front is the same length as the back.

Using the 2.5mm(#1) needles work the border in double rib as for back, finishing with 4 rows in white. Bind off.

• *To make up:* Join the side seams, turn the edge of the armholes and the neck opening ½cm(¼″) under and slipstitch neatly.

To finish the sleeves and the neck: with size 2.5mm(#1) needles and white wool cast on 8 stitches and work 3 strips in stockinette stitch to fit around armholes and neck. Fold these over widthwise and stitch them neatly inside the neck edge and the armholes so that a few millimeters (a fraction of an inch) show on the right side.

Navy blue cardigan (1)
Illustrated in colour on p. 86

Standard: ★★
Tension: 30 stitches and 32 rows to 10cm(4″)
Size: To fit children aged 8-9. The figures in brackets refer to the sizes for 10-11 years and 12-13 years.
Materials: 350g(400g–450g)/12oz(14oz–16oz) of 2-ply yarn in navy blue
1 pair needles size 3mm(#3)
1 crochet hook size 3mm(#C)
5 navy blue buttons
Stitches used: k.3, p.1 rib. Double rib (see p. 58). Shrimp stitch border (see p. 43).

Method
• *Back:* Cast on 108(116–124) stitches and work in k.3, p.1 rib for 40(42–44)cm/16(16½–17)″. Bind off.
• *Fronts:* Cast on 50(58–66) stitches and work in k.3, p.1 rib for 32(34-36)cm/12½(13½–14)″. At neck edge bind off 4 stitches, then 3 stitches, then 2 stitches. Continue in k.3, p.1 rib until front measures same as back. Bind off.

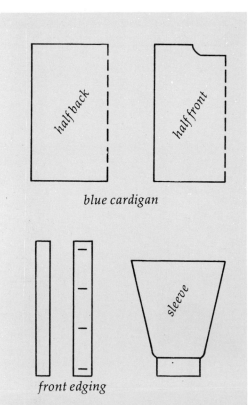

blue cardigan

front edging

Work the other side in the same way, reversing shapings.

- *Sleeves:* Cast on 44(50–54) stitches and work in k.2, p.2 rib for 5cm(2″). Continue in k.3, p.1 rib for 22(26–30)cm/8½(10–11½)″, increasing 1 stitch at each end of every sixth row. Bind off.
- *To make up:* Join shoulder seams. Join side seams, leaving space for sleeves. Join sleeve seams and insert the sleeves.
- *Front borders:* Cast on 140(150–160) stitches and work in double rib (k.2, p.2 rib) for 5(6–7)cm/2(2½–3)″. Make another strip the same size, but with 4 horizontal buttonholes worked over 3 stitches (see p. 45) at 9cm(3½″) intervals.

Stitch borders to front edges using small stitches or back stitch (see p. 143); if the garment is for a girl stitch the buttonhole border to the right-hand edge, to the left-hand edge if it is for a boy.
- *Neck border:* Starting from the right-hand front edge, pick up the neck stitches (see p. 42) with the crochet hook; transfer to a knitting needle and work in double rib for 5cm(2″). Fold the border in half and stitch it to the inside neck edge.
- *Lower border:* Starting from the lower right-hand edge pick up the cast on stitches of the fronts and back with the crochet hook; miss every third stitch so that the border is slightly tighter than the rest of the cardigan. Put the stitches on to a knitting needle and work 12(14–16)cm/5(5½–6)″ in double rib, making a buttonhole 3(3.5–4)cm/1(1¼–1½)″ from the beginning and another 3(3.5–4)cm/1(1¼–1½)″ from the end. Fold the border in half, placing one buttonhole over the other. Work around all the buttonholes in buttonhole stitch (see p. 145). Work along right and left-hand edges in shrimp stitch. Sew on buttons and fold back cuffs.

The garments illustrated in colour on p. 86.

Jacquard socks (2)
Illustrated in colour on p. 86

Standard: ★★★
Tension: 35 stitches and 46 rows to 10cm(4″)
Size: The socks are for children age 13-14 (shoe size 6-6½). The figures in brackets refer to sizes for 11-12 years (shoe size 5-6) and 15-16 (shoe size 6½-7).

Materials: 60g(2½oz) navy linen
30g(1½oz) green linen
30g(1½oz) grey linen
1 set of 4 needles size 2mm(#0)
Elastic 1cm(½″) wide
Stitches used: Stockinette stitch (see p. 57). Jacquard knitting (see pp. 52-3).

Method
- With the navy linen and the set of 4 needles cast on 74(70–78) stitches; work a picot hem (see p. 44) 2cm(1″) wide. Continue in stockinette stitch and Jacquard knitting following the chart for 31(29–33)cm/12(11½–13)″. Begin turning the heel, using stockinette stitch;

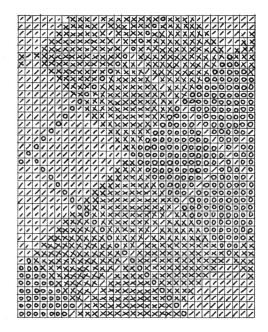

Chart for the Jacquard socks
/ green
× navy
○ grey

work on the 38(34–42) central stitches, choosing one of the methods described on pp. 133-4. The foot is worked entirely in stockinette stitch and Jacquard, and should be 22(20–24)cm/8½(8–9)″ long including the toe; work the toe according to one of the methods described on p. 134.
- *To make up:* Close the toe, using tiny stitches on the wrong side. Insert the elastic through the picot hem.

The garments illustrated in colour on p. 86.

White jumper with light blue and navy stripes (3)
Illustrated in colour on p. 86

Standard: ★★
Tension: 19 stitches and 21 rows to 10cm(4")
Size: The jumper is to fit children aged 10-11. The figures in brackets refer to sizes for 8-9 years and 6-7 years.
Materials: 400g(14oz) white 2-ply Shetland wool
10g(½oz) light blue and navy 2-ply Shetland wool
1 pair knitting needles size 4mm(#6)
1 crochet hook size 4(# F)
Stitches used: Stockinette stitch (see p. 57). Single rib (see p. 57). Shrimp stitch border (see p.43).

Method
● *Back:* Cast on 72(67–62) stitches using one of the invisible methods of casting on described on pp. 30-1; work 3 rows in k.1 slip 1 rib, then work in single rib until border measures 4.5cm(2"). Continue in stockinette stitch, working 2 rows in navy blue, then 2 rows in white and 2 rows in light blue. With white wool continue in stockinette stitch for 35(32–29)cm/14(12½–11½)". Work 2 rows in navy, 2 rows in white and 2 rows in light blue.

Bind off the 22(19–16) central stitches for the neck. Working on both sides separately work 2 rows in white on the 25(24–23) shoulder stitches; bind off.
● *Front:* Cast on 72(67–62) stitches as on back; work 3 rows in k.1 slip 1 rib, then work in single rib until border measures 4.5cm(2"). Change to stockinette stitch and work 2 rows in navy, 2 rows in white and 2 rows in light blue. Continue in white and stockinette stitch for 28(25–22)cm/11(10–8½)". Bind off the 2 central stitches and continue on both sides separately for 6(5–4)cm/2½(2–1½)". Neck shaping: bind off 1 stitch at neck edge for 10 rows. Work the last 6 rows as follows: 2 rows navy, 2 rows white, 2 rows light blue. Bind off.
● *Sleeve:* Cast on 32(30–28) stitches as on back; work 3 rows in k.1 slip 1 rib, then work in single rib until border measures 5.5cm(2¼"). Change to stockinette stitch and work 2 rows in navy, 2 rows in white, 2 rows in light blue. Continue in stockinette stitch and white for 35(32–29)cm/14(12½–11)" increasing 1 stitch at each end of every 6 rows. Work 2 rows in navy, 2 rows in white, 2 rows in light blue, then 2 rows in white. Bind off.
● *To make up:* Stitch the side seams, leaving space for the sleeves. Stitch sleeve seams and across shoulders. Insert sleeves.
● *Neck border:* Cast on 70(68–66) stitches as on back and work 3 rows in k.1 slip 1 rib. Continue in single rib for 5 more rows, then bind off. Stitch the bound off edge of the neck band to the neck shaping.

Using the crochet hook work a row of shrimp stitch around the front opening.

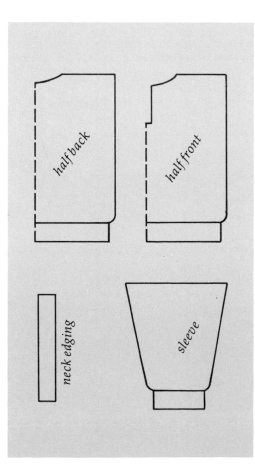

The garments illustrated in
colour on p. 86.

White linen socks (4)
Illustrated in colour on p. 86

Standard: ★★★

Tension: 37 stitches and 56 rows to
10cm(4")

Size: To fit children aged 9-10 (shoe size
3½-4½). The figures in brackets refer to
the sizes for 11-12 years (shoe size 5-6)
and 13-14 years (shoe size 6-6½).

Materials: 50g(60g–70g)/2oz(2½oz–3oz)
white linen twist
1 set of 4 needles size 2mm(#0)
Elastic

Stitches used: Single rib (see p. 57).
Double rib (see p. 58). Stockinette stitch
(see p. 57).

Method

● Using the set of 4 needles and one of
the invisible methods of casting on described on pp. 30-1, cast on 74 stitches
and work in k.1 slip 1 rib for 3.5cm(1½").
Continue in double rib for 24(28–30)cm/
9½(11–12)". Begin turning the heel,
working on the 40(42–44) central stitches
and using one of the methods described
on pp. 113-4. The heel and sole are
worked in stockinette stitch and should
measure 18(20–24)cm/7(8–9½)". The toe
is also worked in stockinette stitch; fol
low one of the methods described on p.
134.

● *To make up:* Close the toe using tiny
stitches on the wrong side. Thread elastic
through the sock border and fasten off.

Jacquard pullover (1)
Illustrated in colour on p. 87

Standard: ★★★

Tension: 37 stitches and 56 rows to
10cm(4")

Size: The pullover is for size 38. The
figures in brackets refer to sizes 36 and 34.

Materials: 250g (200g–150g) /9oz (7oz–
5oz) green sport yarn
70g (60g–50g) /2½oz (2¼oz–2oz) light
beige sport yarn
70g (60g–50g) /2½oz (2¼oz–2oz) dark
beige sport yarn
1 pair needles size 4mm(#6)
1 crochet hook, size 4(# F)

Stitches used: Double rib (see p. 58).
Stockinette stitch (see p. 57). Jacquard
knitting (see pp. 52-3).

Method

● *Back:* using green wool cast on 80(75–
70) stitches and work 5cm(2") in double
rib.

Change to stockinette stitch and follow
the Jacquard chart. When the work measures 40cm(16"), bind off for the
armholes: on either side bind off 3 stitches, then 2 stitches, then 1 stitch. Continue
in stockinette stitch for 22(20–18)cm/
8½(8–7)". Bind off the 26(23–20) central
stitches and continue on both sides
separately: work 2 rows and bind off the
24(23–22) shoulder stitches.

Chart for the Jacquard pullover
× green
○ light beige
● dark beige

● *Front:* Using green wool cast on
80(75–70) stitches and work 5cm(2") in
double rib. Continue in stockinette stitch
and Jacquard knitting, following the
chart above, until work measures 40(38–
36)cm/16(15–14)".

To shape armholes bind off 4 stitches,
then 3 stitches, then 2 stitches on each
side. Bind off the 3 central stitches for the
V-neck and continue on both sides separately. Decrease 1 stitch every third row at

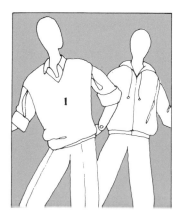

The garments illustrated in
colour on p. 87.

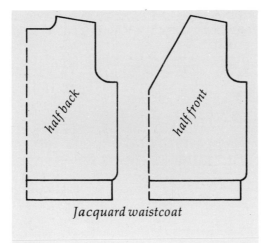

Jacquard waistcoat

neck edge until 24(23–22) stitches remain.

Continue without shaping until front measures same as back. Bind off.

● *To make up:* Join side seams and shoulder seams.

Using the crochet hook and green wool, pick up the stitches around the armholes starting from the front armhole shaping. Work 2cm(1″) in double rib.

Pick up the stitches around the V-neck, starting from the point of the V and working up the right-hand side. Work 2cm(1″) in double rib.

Stitch the borders together at the point of the V and under the arms.

Jacket with hood (2)
Illustrated in colour on p. 87

Standard: ★★

Tension: 24 stitches and 24 rows to 10cm(4″)

Size: Men's size 40. The figures in brackets refer to sizes 38 and 42.

Materials: 800g(750g–850g)/28oz(26oz–30oz) beige camel hair
1 pair needles size 5mm(#8)
Beige lining material to match camel hair
1 zipper 58cm(23″) long, open at both ends.
It is advisable to line this jacket.

Stitches used: Fisherman's rib (see p. 58).

Method

● *Back:* Cast on 146(140–152) stitches and work in fisherman's rib for 66(64–68)cm/26(25–27)″. Bind off.

● *Fronts:* Cast on 62(59–65) stitches and work in fisherman's rib for 62cm(24½″). To shape neck, decrease 3 stitches at neck edge 6 times. Continue until front measures the same as back. Bind off.

Work the other side in the same way, reversing shapings.

● *Sleeves:* Cast on 80(78–82) stitches and work in fisherman's rib for 53(50–56)cm/21(20–22)″, increasing at each end of every eighth row; bind off.

● *Hood:* Cast on 178 stitches and work in fisherman's rib for 25cm(9″). Bind off.

● *To make up:* Join side seams: 13cm(5″) from bottom edge, leave a space measuring 12cm(4½″). Continue the seam, leaving an opening for the sleeves.

Fold the hood strip in half and stitch along one of the long sides on the wrong side. Make a 3cm(1¼″) hem on the other side and stitch using back stitch (see p. 143). Stitch the short sides of the hood to the neck edge.

The garments illustrated in colour on p. 87.

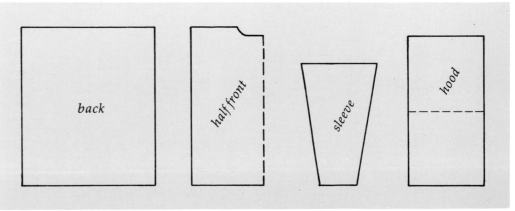

back   half front   sleeve   hood

At the lower edge and the sleeve edges of the jacket fold back 3cm(1¼") and stitch using back stitch.

With the lining material make two pocket linings, 12cm × 12cm (5" × 5") and insert them into the gaps left in the side seams, stitching them inside the seam allowance. Make two double plaited cords (see p. 139), each measuring 150cm(59") and thread them through the hem around the hood and around the lower edge of the jacket.

Stitch the zipper to the two fronts. Line the whole jacket, including the hood.

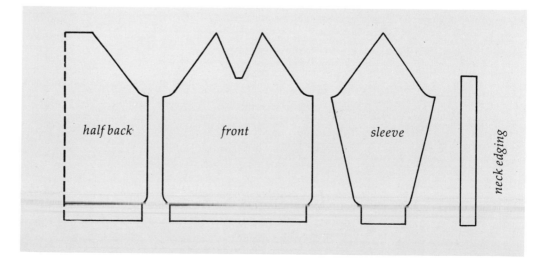

The garments illustrated in colour on p. 88.

Blue V-neck pullover with squares (1)
Illustrated in colour on p. 88

Standard: ★★
Tension: 20 stitches and 24 rows to 10cm(4")
Size: Men's size 34. The figures in brackets refer to sizes 36 and 38.
Materials: 500g(550g–600g)/17oz(18oz–20oz) blue sport yarn
1 pair needles size 4mm(#6)
Stitches used: Single rib (see p. 57). Stockinette stitch (see p. 57).

Method
● *Back:* Cast on 85(91–97) stitches using one of the invisible methods of casting on described on pp. 30-1; work in k.1 slip 1 rib for 3 rows.

Continue in single rib for 6.5cm(2½"), then change to stockinette stitch and work 40(42–44)cm/16(16½–17)". To shape raglan armholes bind off 3 stitches, then 2 stitches at each side. Continue, decreasing 1 stitch at each end of every row until work measures 22(23–24)cm/8½(9–9½)" from armholes. Bind off remaining stitches.

● *Front:* Cast on 90(96–102) stitches as on back; work 3 rows in k.1 slip 1 rib. Continue in single rib for 6.5cm(2½"), then work 40(42–44)cm/16(16½–17)" in square pattern as follows: for the first 20 rows: *15(16–17) purl, 15(16–17) knit*; for the following 20 rows: *15(16–17) knit, 15(16–17) purl*. Repeat first 20 rows, then second 20 rows and so on.

Shape raglan armholes as described for back. After 7(8–9)cm/2½(3–3½)" of raglan shaping bind off the 10 central stitches for the V-neck. Continue on both sides separately, maintaining raglan shaping. At the same time shape V-neck, decreasing 1 stitch at neck edge on every third row until front measures same as back.

● *Sleeves:* Cast on 40(44–48) stitches as on back; work 3 rows in k.1 slip 1 rib. Continue in single rib until work measures 7.5cm(3"), then work 35(37–39)cm/13½(14–15)" in stockinette stitch. Shape raglan top as described for back.

● *To make up:* Join shoulder and side seams. Join sleeve seams and insert sleeves.

For neck border, cast on 106(110–114) stitches as on back; work 3 rows in k.1

half back   front   sleeve   neck edging

slip 1 rib. Continue in single rib until work measures 3cm(1¼"). Bind off.

Stitch one of the ends of this strip across the 10 stitches at center of V, then, working from right to left and using back stitch (see p. 143), stitch the bound off edge right around the neck edge. Stitch the other end of the strip under the first end.

The garments illustrated in colour on p. 88.

Grey and dark red pullover (2)
Illustrated in colour on p. 88

Standard: ★★
Tension: 25 stitches and 31 rows to 10cm(4")
Size: Men's size 36. The figures in brackets refer to sizes 38 and 40.
Materials: 250g(300g–350g)/9oz(10½–12oz) grey wool
250g(300g–350g)/9oz(10½oz–12oz) dark red wool
1 pair needles size 3.5mm(#4)
1 pair needles size 4mm(#6)
1 crochet hook size 3.5mm(# E)
Stitches used: Stockinette stitch (see p. 57). Single rib (see p. 57). Jacquard knitting (see pp. 52-3).

Method
• *Back:* With grey wool and needles size 3.5mm(#4) cast on 110(116–122) stitches using one of the invisible methods of casting on described on pp. 30-1; work 3 rows in k.1 slip 1 rib. Continue in single rib until work measures 9cm(3½").

Change to size 4mm(#6) needles and stockinette stitch, working the Jacquard pattern according to the chart; work 43(44–45)cm/17(17¼–17¾)", then decrease for the armholes, 2 stitches at each end of alternate rows 4 times. Continue in grey wool until work measures 18(19–20)cm/7(7½–8)" from armholes, then shape shoulders by binding off 3 stitches at each end of alternate rows 10 times. Bind off remaining stitches.
• *Front:* With grey wool and size 3.5mm(#4) needles cast on 110(116–122) stitches as on back. Work 3 rows in k.1 slip 1 rib. Continue in single rib until

work measures 9cm(3½"). Change to size 4mm(#6) needles and stockinette stitch, working the Jacquard pattern according to the chart; work 43(44–45)cm/17(17¼–17¾)", then decrease for armholes, 2 stitches at each end of alternate rows 4 times. Continue in grey wool until work measures 12.5cm(5") from armholes.

Shape neck by binding off the 20 central stitches. Working each side separately, bind off 2 stitches at neck edge on alternate rows 9 times. Continue in stockinette stitch until front armholes measure same as back armholes. Bind off.
• *Sleeves:* With grey wool and needles size 3.5mm(#4) cast on 50(52–54) stitches as on back; work 3 rows in k.1 slip 1 rib. Continue in single rib until work measures 8cm(3"). Change to size 4mm(#6) needles and stockinette stitch, working the Jacquard pattern according to the chart, and increasing 1 stitch at

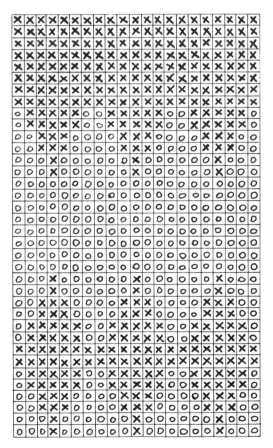

Chart for the grey and dark red pullover

× dark red
○ grey

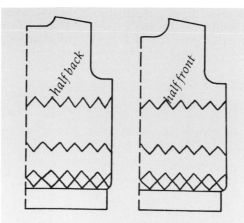

grey and burgundy sweater

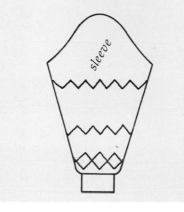

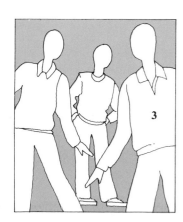

The garments illustrated in colour on p. 88.

Materials: 500g(450g–400g)/18oz(16oz–14oz) grey Shetland wool
150g(120g–100g)/5oz(4oz–3½oz) blue Shetland wool
1 pair needles size 4mm(#6)
Stitches used: Single rib (see p. 57). Stockinette stitch (see p. 57). Jacquard knitting (see pp. 52-3).

Method
● *Back:* With blue wool cast on 118(112–106) stitches, using one of the invisible methods of casting on described on pp. 30-1; work 3 rows in k.1 slip 1 rib.

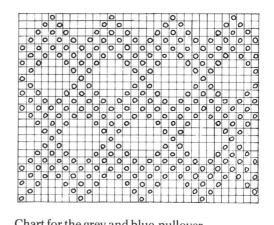

Chart for the grey and blue pullover
○ blue
□ grey

Change to grey wool and single rib and continue until work measures 3cm(1″).

Change to stockinette stitch and work 44(41–38)cm/17(16–15)″. Shape arm-holes by binding off 4 stitches, then 3 stitches, then 2 stitches on each side. Work 20(18–16)cm/8(7–6½)″ from arm-hole shaping. Bind off.
● *Front:* Cast on 118(112–106) stitches as on back using blue wool and work 3 rows in k.1 slip 1 rib. Change to grey wool and single rib and continue until work measures 3cm(1″).

Change to stockinette stitch and Jac-quard knitting, following the chart; work 44(41–38)cm/17(16–15)″.

Shape armhole by binding off 4 stitch-es, then 3 stitches, then 2 stitches on each side. Bind off the 12 central stitches for the V-neck and continue each side separ-ately. Decrease 1 stitch at neck edge on alternate rows until front measures same as back to shoulder; bind off shoulder stitches.

each end of every sixth row. When work measures 40(42–44)cm/16(16½–17)″, shape top by decreasing 2 stitches at each end of alternate rows 3 times. Continue to decrease 1 stitch at each end of every alternate row until 8 stitches remain. Bind off.
● *To make up:* Join shoulder, side and sleeve seams. Insert sleeves.

Using the crochet hook pick up the stitches around neck (see p. 42) and with needles size 3.5mm(#4) work 7.5cm(3″) in single rib. Fold the border in half and slip stitch neatly to inside.

Grey and blue pullover (3)
Illustrated in colour on p. 88

Standard: ★★★
Tension: 22 stitches and 34 rows to 10cm(4″)
Size: Men's size 38. The figures in brack-ets refer to sizes 36 and 34.

The garments illustrated in colour on p. 105.

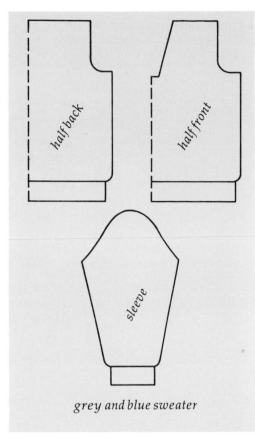

half back

half front

sleeve

grey and blue sweater

• *Sleeves:* Cast on 58(52–46) stitches using blue wool as on back; work 3 rows in k.1 slip 1 rib. Change to grey wool and single rib and continue until work measures 6cm(2½").

Continue in grey, changing to stockinette stitch and increase 1 stitch at each end of every eighth row until work measures 38(36–34)cm/15(14–13½)".

Shape top by binding off 4 stitches, then 3 stitches, then 2 stitches on each side. Continue decreasing 1 stitch at each end of every row until 25(22–20) stitches remain; bind off.

• *To make up:* Join shoulder, side and sleeve seams; insert sleeves.

For the neck border, cast on 200 stitches using blue wool as on back; work in k.1 slip 1 rib for 3 rows. Change to grey wool and single rib and work until border measures 3cm(1"). Bind off.

Using back stitch (see p. 143), stitch one end of the border to the 12 bound off stitches of the V-neck. Working from right to left, stitch the bound off edge of

the border right around the neck edge; stitch the other end of the border underneath the first so that it cannot be seen.

White sweater-vest with double seed stitch pattern (1)
Illustrated in colour on p. 105.

Standard: ★★
Tension: 24 stitches and 32 rows to 10cm(4")
Size: Women's size 36" bust. The figures in brackets refer to sizes 34 and 38.
Materials: 280g(250g–300g)/10oz(9oz–11oz) white 3-ply wool
1 pair needles size 2.5mm(#1)
5 white buttons
Stitches used: Garter stitch stripe pattern (see below). Double seed stitch (see p. 60). Garter stitch (see p. 57).

Method
• *Back:* Cast on 110(104–116) stitches and work in garter stitch for 1.5cm(½"). Continue in double seed stitch for 4cm(1½"), then change to garter stitch stripe pattern worked as follows: 3 rows knit, 3 rows purl. Work 31(28–34)cm/12(11–13½)".

Work 2cm(¾"), working the first and last 16 stitches in double seed stitch and the central stitches in garter stitch stripe pattern.

Now work 1.5cm(½"), working the first and last 16 stitches as follows: 10 stitches in garter stitch, 6 stitches in double seed stitch; 6 stitches in double seed stitch and 10 stitches in garter stitch.

To shape armholes, bind off 5 stitches at each side, then work 18cm(7"), working the stitches as they appear on the needle (5 stitches in garter stitch, 6 stitches in double seed stitch, etc.). To shape shoulders, bind off 4 stitches at shoulder edge 7 times. Bind off.

• *Fronts:* Cast on 65 stitches and work 1.5cm(½") in garter stitch. Continue in double seed stitch, working 5 stitches in garter stitch at the buttonhole edge. At the start of the double seed stitch work one vertical buttonhole over 2 rows (see p. 45) in the garter stitch border. The other buttonholes should be worked at 8cm(3") intervals. When 4cm(1½") of double seed stitch have been worked

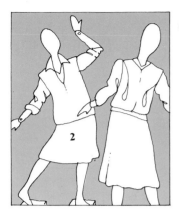

The garments illustrated in colour on p. 105.

change to garter stitch stripe pattern (3 rows knit, 3 rows purl), but continuing to work a garter stitch border of 5 stitches, and a double seed stitch border of 12 stitches; work 31(28–34)cm/12(11–13½)". Begin to shape the V-neck: decrease 1 stitch on alternate rows inside the garter stitch border. Either continue to work the 12 following stitches in double seed stitch, or work the rest of the row in garter stitch stripe pattern.

At the same time, on the other side, work 22 stitches in double seed stitch for reversing shapings.

● *To make up:* Join shoulder seams and side seams. Join the two garter stitch borders and stitch along the back of the neck. Sew on buttons.

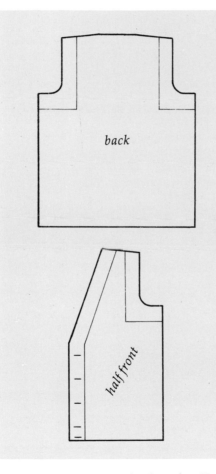

2cm(¾"). Then, continuing the V-neck shaping, shape armholes at the same measurement as back armholes by binding off 11 stitches at each side. Now at armhole edge work 5 stitches in garter stitch, and 6 stitches in double seed stitch. When front measures same as back to shoulders bind off all the stitches except for the 5 border stitches at neck. Work 8cm(3") on these stitches. Bind off.

Work the other front in the same way,

Dark red skirt with sunray pleats (2)

Illustrated in colour on p. 105.

Standard: ★★
Tension: 23 stitches and 30 rows to 10cm(4")
Size: Women's size 38. The figures in brackets refer to sizes 36 and 40.
Materials: 400g(350g-450g) dark red 3-ply worsted
1 pair needles size 3mm(#3)
Waist elastic, width 2cm(¾")
Stitches used: Stockinette stitch; reversed stockinette stitch (see p. 57).

Method

The skirt is worked in two identical halves, beginning from the lower edge.

Cast on 192(186-200) stitches and work in k.8, p.8 rib. Work 57(54–60)cm/22½(21¼–23½)", gradually decreasing the purl stitches (see instructions for sunray pleats on p. 50) until only 1 purl stitch remains between each group of 8

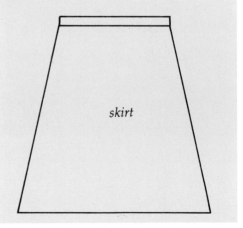

knit stitches. Work 11cm(4¼"). Bind off.

● *To make up:* Join the front and back seams together neatly. To make the waistband turn the edge over 3cm(1½"), and slip-stitch around, leaving a gap for inserting elastic. Thread the elastic through and join ends, then complete the slip-stitching around the waist.

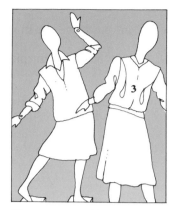

The garments illustrated in colour on p. 105.

Pink sweater with butterfly pattern (3)

Illustrated in colour on p. 105

Standard: ★★
Tension: 23 stitches and 40 rows to 10cm(4″)
Size: Women's size 34. The figures in brackets refer to sizes 36 and 38 respectively.
Materials: 300g(350g–400g)/10½oz (12oz–14oz) pink 3-ply worsted
1 pair needles size 3mm(#3)
1 crochet hook, size 3mm(#C)
4 pink buttons
Stitches used: stockinette stitch (see p. 57). Butterfly pattern (see p. 75). Garter stitch (see p. 57). Single rib (see p. 57).

Method

• *Back:* Cast on 106(114–122) stitches using one of the invisible methods of casting on described on pp. 30–1; work 3 rows in k.1 slip 1 rib. Continue in single rib until work measures 4cm(1½″). Change to stockinette stitch and work 36(39–42) cm/14(15–16½)″.
Shape armholes by binding off 3 stitches, then 1 stitch on each side. Continue in stockinette stitch for 14(15–16cm)/5½(6–6½)″. Shape shoulders by binding off 3 stitches at the beginning of every row until 33(36–39) stitches have been bound off on either side; 32(34–36) stitches remain on the needle. Shape back of neck by binding off first the 10 central stitches, then the 11(12–13) side stitches.
• *Front:* Cast on 108(116–124) stitches as on back; work 3 rows in k.1 slip 1 rib. Continue in single rib until work measures 4cm(1½″). Change to stockinette stitch and work 23cm(9″). Start working in butterfly pattern and work 4cm(1½″), or 2 lines of butterflies.
Divide the front as follows: 56(60–64) stitches for the right-hand side and 52(56–60) for the left. Continue each side separately, beginning with the right-hand side as follows: 50(54–58) stitches in butterfly stitch, 6 stitches in garter stitch for the buttonhole border. When the garter stitch border measures 5cm(2″) work a baby clothes buttonhole (see p. 45). Work 4cm(1½″) so that the length to the armhole measures the same as the back, and shape armhole as follows: bind

off 4 stitches, 3 stitches, then 2 stitches at armhole edge. Working 2 more buttonholes at 5cm(2″) intervals, continue until front measures 43cm(16¾″).
Begin neck shaping by binding off the 6 stitches of the garter stitch border. Then at neck edge, bind off at the beginning of each row 3 stitches twice, then 1 stitch until the same number of stitches remain as for back shoulder. Bind off all the stitches.

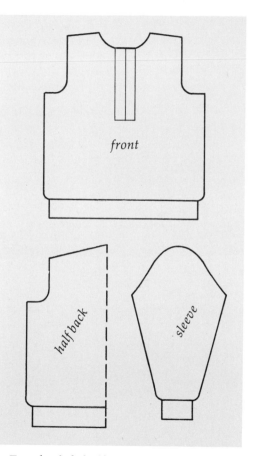

For the left half, cast on 6 stitches for garter stitch border and work in the same way, reversing shapings.
• *Sleeves:* Cast on 46(52–58) stitches as on back; work 3 rows in k.1 slip 1 rib. Continue in single rib until work measures 6cm(2½″), then change to butterfly pattern and work 5cm(2″) or 3 rows of butterflies, increasing 1 stitch at each end of every fourth row. Then continue in stockinette stitch increasing at each end of every sixth row. Work 32cm(12½″).
To shape top bind off 4 stitches, then 3 stitches, then 1 stitch on each side.

Continue, decreasing 1 stitch at each end until 22(28–34) stitches remain. Bind off one third of the stitches at the beginning of the next 3 rows.

● *To make up:* Join shoulder and side seams. Join sleeve seams and insert sleeves. Using a crochet hook pick up stitches around neck edge (see p. 42), beginning at the right-hand edge, and working around the right front, the back, and the left front. Work 6 rows in garter stitch. On the second row work a buttonhole to match the buttonholes on the front border. Bind off. Sew on buttons and stitch the 6 cast on stitches at the base of the left front opening to the garter stitch border of the right front, using small stitches.

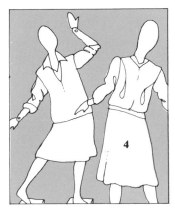

The garments illustrated in colour on p. 105.

Purple striped skirt (4)
Illustrated in colour on p. 105

Standard: ★★
Tension: 18 stitches and 31 rows to 10cm(4″).
Size: Women's size 34-36. The figures in brackets refer to size 38-40.
Materials: Shetland wool is used for this skirt. You will need:
270g(330g)/10oz(12oz) purple
30g(1oz) yellow
30g(1oz) grey
30g(1oz) light grey
1 pair needles size 4mm(#6)
Waist elastic, 2cm(¾″) wide
Stitches used: Stockinette stitch (see p. 57). Single rib (see p. 57).

The garments illustrated in colour on p. 106.

waistband

skirt

Method
The skirt is knitted in one piece starting from the waist.

Cast on 171(189) stitches with purple wool and work 13(15)cm/5(6)″ in k.9, p.9 rib.

Increase 1 stitch on each panel of the sunray pleats before each band of stripes. Work the first as follows: 2 rows light grey, 2 purple, 2 grey, 2 purple, 2 yellow, 4 purple, 2 yellow, 2 purple, 2 grey, 2 purple, 2 light grey.

Continue in purple for 6(8)cm/2¼(3)″, then work second striped band: 2 rows yellow, 2 purple, 2 grey, 2 purple, 2 light grey, 4 purple, 2 light grey, 2 purple, 2 grey, 2 purple, 2 yellow.

Continue in purple for 6(8)cm/2¼(3)″, then work third striped band: 2 rows grey, 2 purple, 2 yellow, 2 purple, 2 light grey, 4 purple, 2 grey, 2 purple, 2 yellow, 2 purple, 2 light grey.

Continue in purple and work 13cm(5″) then bind off.

● *To make up:* Join the open side. For the waistband, cast on 122(134) stitches and work in single rib for 6cm(2¼″). Bind off. Fold the border and stitch to waistline. Insert the elastic and fasten ends.

Yellow linen vest (1)
Illustrated in colour on p. 106

Standard: ★★
Tension: 35 stitches and 45 rows to 10cm(4″).
Size: Women's size 40. The figures in brackets refer to sizes 38 and 36.
Materials: 200g (180g–150g) /7oz (6oz–5oz) yellow linen
1 pair needles size 2mm(#0)
Crochet hook, size 2mm(#0 steel)
Stitches used: Double rib (see p. 58). Stockinette stitch (see p. 57). Simple cable (see p. 62).

Method
● *Back:* Cast on 150(140–130) stitches and work in double rib for 6cm(2¼″). Continue in stockinette stitch for 36(34–32)cm/14(13½–12½)″.

Shape armholes by binding off 3 stitches twice, 2 stitches twice, 1 stitch twice on each side. Continue in stockinette stitch for 20(19–18)cm/8(7½–7)″.

The garments illustrated in colour on p. 106.

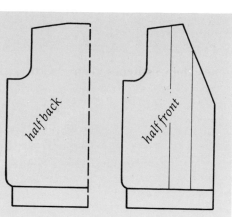

yellow linen waistcoat

To shape shoulders bind off 14(13–12) stitches 3 times on each side. Bind off the remaining 42(38–34) stitches.

● *Right front:* Cast on 76(70–64) stitches and work in double rib for 6cm(2¼"). Continue in stockinette stitch on the first and last 25(22–19) stitches. The 26 central stitches are worked as follows: the first 10 and last 10 are worked in simple cable stitch (see p. 62). The central 6 stitches are also worked in simple cable, crossing 3 stitches rather than 2 every 10 rows.

Continue this pattern for 18(16-14)cm/ 7(6¼–5½)", then begin neck shaping: decrease 1 stitch at neck edge on every fourth row. Begin armhole shaping when the front measures the same as the back, working as for back armhole shaping. Work shoulders as for back.

The left front is worked in the same way, reversing shapings and without cable band.

● *To make up:* Join side and shoulder seams. Using the crochet hook pick up the stitches (see p. 42) along the front edge, neck edge and back of neck, beginning at the bottom right. Work 5cm(2") in double rib. Pick up the stitches around the armholes and work 4cm(1½") in double rib.

Fold all the borders in half and slip-stitch on wrong side. On the right front border cut 4 vertical buttonholes at 5cm(2") intervals; each buttonhole should be 6 stitches long. Finish the buttonholes with buttonhole stitch.

Sew the buttons to the left-hand front border to match buttonholes.

Short-sleeved blue cotton sweater (2)

Illustrated in colour on p. 106.

Standard: ★★
Tension: 33 stitches and 44 rows to 10cm(4")
Size: The sweater is to fit women's size 36. The figures in brackets refer to sizes 38 and 40.
Materials: 150g (180g–200g) /5oz (6oz–7oz) cotton no. 8 in blue.
1 pair needles size 2mm(#0)
1 pair needles size 2.5mm(#1)
1 crochet hook, size 2mm(#0 steel)
Stitches used: Garter stitch (see p. 57). Simple eyelet pattern (see p. 77). Single rib (see p. 57).

Method
● *Back:* Using size 2mm(#0) needles cast on 130(136–142) stitches and work 5

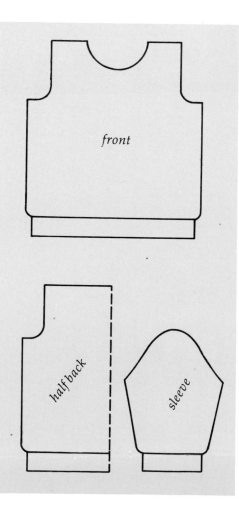

front

half back

sleeve

rows in garter stitch. Change to size 2.5mm(#1) needles and simple eyelet pattern and work 40(42–44)cm/15¾(16½–17¼)". Shape armholes by binding off 5 stitches, then 3 stitches, then 2 stitches at each side. Continue in simple eyelet pattern for another 20(21–22)cm/8(8½–8¾)"; bind off.

● *Front:* Using size 2mm(#0) needles cast on 140(146–152) stitches and work 5 rows in garter stitch. Change to size 2.5mm(#1) needles and work in simple eyelet pattern until front measures same as back to armholes.

Shape armholes by binding off 6 stitches, then 3 stitches, then 2 stitches at each side. Work 7(8–9)cm/2¾(3¼–3½)".

To shape neck bind off the 20(26–32) central stitches, then continue on both sides separately. At neck edge bind off 10 stitches, then 6 stitches. Work until front measures same as back to shoulder. Bind off.

● *Sleeves:* Using size 2mm(#0) needles, cast on 80(90–100) stitches and work in single rib for 4cm(1½"). Change to size 2.5mm(#1) needles and work 5(6–7)cm/2(2½–2¾)" in simple eyelet pattern, increasing 1 stitch at both ends on every fourth row.

Shape top by binding off 5 stitches, 3 stitches, then 2 stitches at each side. Continue, decreasing 1 stitch at each end of every row until 30 stitches remain. Bind off 10 stitches 3 times.

● *To make up:* Join side seams and shoulder seams. Join sleeve seams and insert sleeves.

Using the crochet hook pick up the stitches (see p. 42) around the back of the neck, transfer them to needles size 2mm(#0) and work 5 rows in garter stitch. Then pick up stitches around front of neck, transfer them to needles size 2mm(#0) and work 5 rows in garter stitch.

Join the seams of the neck border at the shoulders.

Fuchsia silk cardigan (3)
Illustrated in colour on p. 106

Standard: ★★
Tension: 24 stitches and 35 rows to 10cm(4")
Size: Women's size 34. The figures in brackets refer to sizes 36 and 38.
Materials: 300g (320g-350g) /10½oz (11oz–12oz) fuchsia silk
1 pair needles size 3mm(#3)
Crochet hook size 3mm(#C)
Stitches used: Stockinette stitch (see p. 57). Single rib (see p. 57). Shrimp stitch border (see p. 43).

Method
● *Back:* Cast on 110(130–150) stitches using one of the invisible methods of

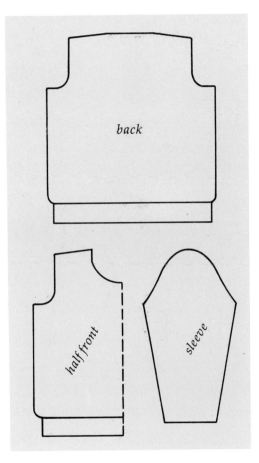

casting on described on pp. 30-1, and work 3 rows in k.1 slip 1 rib. Continue in single rib for 2.5cm(1"), then change to stockinette stitch and work 38(40–42)cm/15(15¾–16½)"

Shape armholes by binding off 3 stitches, then 2 stitches, then 1 stitch at each side; continue in stockinette stitch for 18(19–20)cm/7(7½–8)". Begin shoulder shaping by binding off 5 stitches at the beginning of every row until 30(35–40)

The garments illustrated in colour on p. 106.

stitches have been bound off on each side; 38(48–58) stitches remain.

Bind off the 14(16–20) central stitches first, then the 12(16–19) side stitches.

● *Fronts:* Cast on 55(65–75) stitches as on back. Work 3 rows in k.1 slip 1 rib. Continue in single rib for 2.5cm(1″), then change to stockinette stitch and work 38(40–42)cm/15(15¾–16½)″. Work armhole as for back.

Continue in stockinette stitch for 10cm(4″), then shape neck. Bind off 4(6–8) stitches, 3(5–7) stitches, 2 stitches, then 1 stitch at neck edge. Continue until front measures same as back to shoulder shaping and shape shoulders to match, binding off the 33(37–41) stitches 5 at a time at the armhole edge.

Work the other front in the same way, reversing shapings.

● *Sleeves:* Cast on 54(64–74) stitches and work in single rib (see p. 57) for 4cm(1½″). Work 34(36–38)cm/13½(14–15)″ in stockinette stitch increasing 1 stitch at each end of every tenth row.

Shape top as for back armhole shaping, then continue without further shaping until sleeve top measures 16(18–20)cm/7(7½–8)″.

● *To make up:* Join side and shoulder seams. Join sleeve seams and insert sleeves, gathering the sleeve at the top to fit. Turn in front border 5mm(¼″) and slip-stitch into place. Work a shrimp stitch crochet border around neck edge.

Make two single cords (see p. 138) and stitch to neck edge as fastenings.

The garments illustrated in colour on p. 106.

Fuchsia silk top (4)
Illustrated in colour on p. 106

Standard: ★
Tension: 24 stitch and 35 rows to 10cm(4″)
Size: To fit size 34. The figures in brackets refer to sizes 36 and 38.
Materials: 100g(130g–150g)/4oz(4½oz–5oz) fuchsia silk
1 pair needles size 3mm(#3)
Elastic 1.5cm(½″) wide
Stitches used: Stockinette stitch (see p. 57). Single rib (see p. 57).

Method
● *Back:* Begin at the top. Cast on 100(110–120) stitches and make a simple hem (see p. 44) 2cm(¾″) deep. Continue in stockinette stitch for 40(42–44)cm/16(16½–17)″, then work 2cm(¾″) in single rib. Bind off using the invisible method (see p. 31).

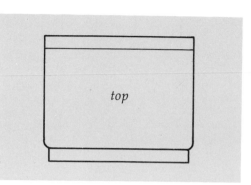

● *Front:* Worked exactly the same as the back.
● *To make up:* Join side seams and thread elastic through top hem.

White cowl-neck pullover with lurex pattern (1)
Illustrated in colour on p. 107

Standard ★★
Tension: 18 stitches and 20 rows to 10cm(4″)
Size: Women's size 36-38. The figures in brackets refer to sizes 38-40.
Materials: 250g (300g) /9oz (10½oz) white mohair
50g(2oz) silver lurex thread
1 pair needles size 3mm(#3)
1 set of 4 needles size 3mm(#3)
1 crochet hook size 3mm(#C)
Stitches used: Garter stitch (see p. 57). Stockinette stitch (see p. 57). Basket stitch (see p. 61).

Method
● *Back:* Cast on 90(100) stitches in mohair and work 3 cm(1¼″) in garter stitch. Join the lurex with the mohair and work 1 row in garter stitch. Using mohair alone finish the border by working 3cm(1¼″) in garter stitch.

Change to stockinette stitch and work 3cm(1¼") then join in the lurex and work a row of eyelets as follows: k.2, *k.2 tog, yarn around needle*, k.2. Keeping yarns together, purl 1 row, then work 3cm(1¼") in mohair only.

Combine the yarns again and work a row of eyelets and a purl row as described above. Continue in mohair and basket stitch for 6cm(2½").

Work the row of eyelets and the purl row with mohair and lurex, then work 3cm(1¼") in mohair and stockinette stitch. Continue, alternating the eyelets in mohair and lurex with 3cm(1¼") in stockinette stitch and mohair for a further 35(40)cm/13¾(15¾)". Bind off.

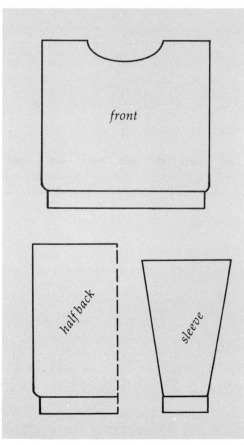
front

half back

sleeve

• *Front:* Work as for back until work measures 46(51)cm/18(20)", then shape neck as follows. Bind off the 10 central stitches and finish both sides separately: decrease at neck edge 3 stitches, 2 stitches, then 1 stitch 3 times. When work measures same as back, bind off shoulders.

• *Sleeves:* Cast on 40(45) stitches and

work 3cm(1¼") in garter stitch; join in lurex and work 1 row in garter stitch. Continue in mohair alone and work 3cm(1¼") in garter stitch.

Work pattern exactly as for back, increasing 1 stitch at each end of every 6 rows; work 40(44)cm/15¾(17¼)". Bind off.

• *To make up:* Join shoulder and side seams leaving a gap for the sleeves. Join sleeve seams and insert sleeves.

Using the crochet hook pick up the stitches (see p. 42) around the neck and transfer to the set of 4 needles. Work 3cm(1¼") in stockinette stitch and mohair, then join in the lurex and work a row of eyelets and a purl row as described for back; continue, alternating 3cm(1¼") of stockinette stitch in mohair and eyelets in mohair and lurex for 16cm(6¼"). Work 2 rows in mohair and garter stitch; bind off.

Jacquard jacket in handspun wool (2)
Illustrated in colour on p. 107

Standard: ★★
Tension: 19 stitches and 20 rows to 10cm(4")
Size: Women's size 36. The figures in brackets refer to sizes 38 and 40.
Materials: The wool used for this jacket was handspun and dyed with vegetable dyes.
300g(350g–400g)/10½oz(12oz–14oz) orange handspun wool
70g(100g–130g)/2½oz(3½oz–4oz) pink
70g(100g–130g)/2½oz(3½oz–4oz) yellow
70g(100g–130g)/2½oz(3½oz–4oz) lilac
70g(100g–130g)/2½oz(3½oz–4oz) sage green
1 pair needles size 3mm(#3)
1 crochet hook, size 3.5mm(#E)
Stitches used: Garter stitch (see p. 57). Jacquard knitting (see pp. 52–3).

Method
• *Back:* Cast on 80(90–100) stitches with orange wool and work 6cm(2½") in garter stitch, changing colour every 2 rows and using all 5 colours.

Continue in stockinette stitch and Jacquard knitting, following the chart care-

The garments illustrated in colour on p. 107.

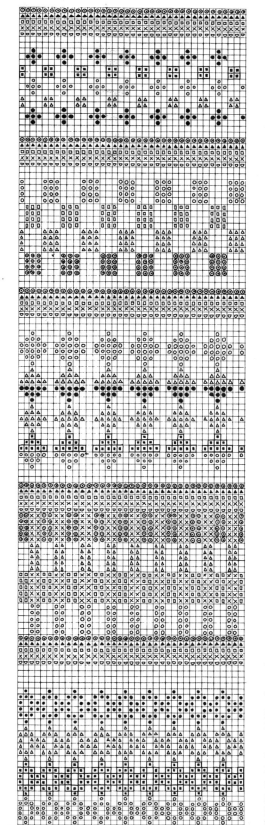

Beginning of armhole shaping →

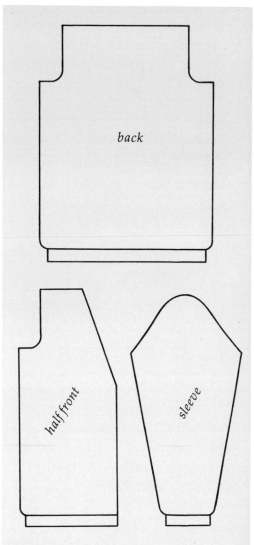

back

half front

sleeve

Chart for the Jacquard jacket
in handspun wool

☐ orange background
△ pink
○ yellow
● lilac
⊡ sage green
☐ sage green garter stitch
☐ orange garter stitch
× orange garter stitch
⊙ lilac garter stitch
▲ pink garter stitch
▽ yellow garter stitch

fully until you reach the row where
armhole shaping is marked. Shape
armholes by binding off at each side 2
stitches twice, then 1 stitch.

Continue in stockinette stitch and Jacquard until chart has been worked
through. Bind off.

● *Fronts:* Cast on 40(45–50) stitches
with orange wool and work 6cm(2½″) in
garter stitch, changing colour every 2
rows and using all 5 colours.

Continue in stockinette stitch and Jacquard; work 30cm(12″) then shape V-
neck by decreasing 1 stitch at neck edge
every 6 rows. At the same time, when you
reach the row where armhole shaping is
indicated on the chart, shape armholes by
binding off 3 stitches, then 2 stitches, then

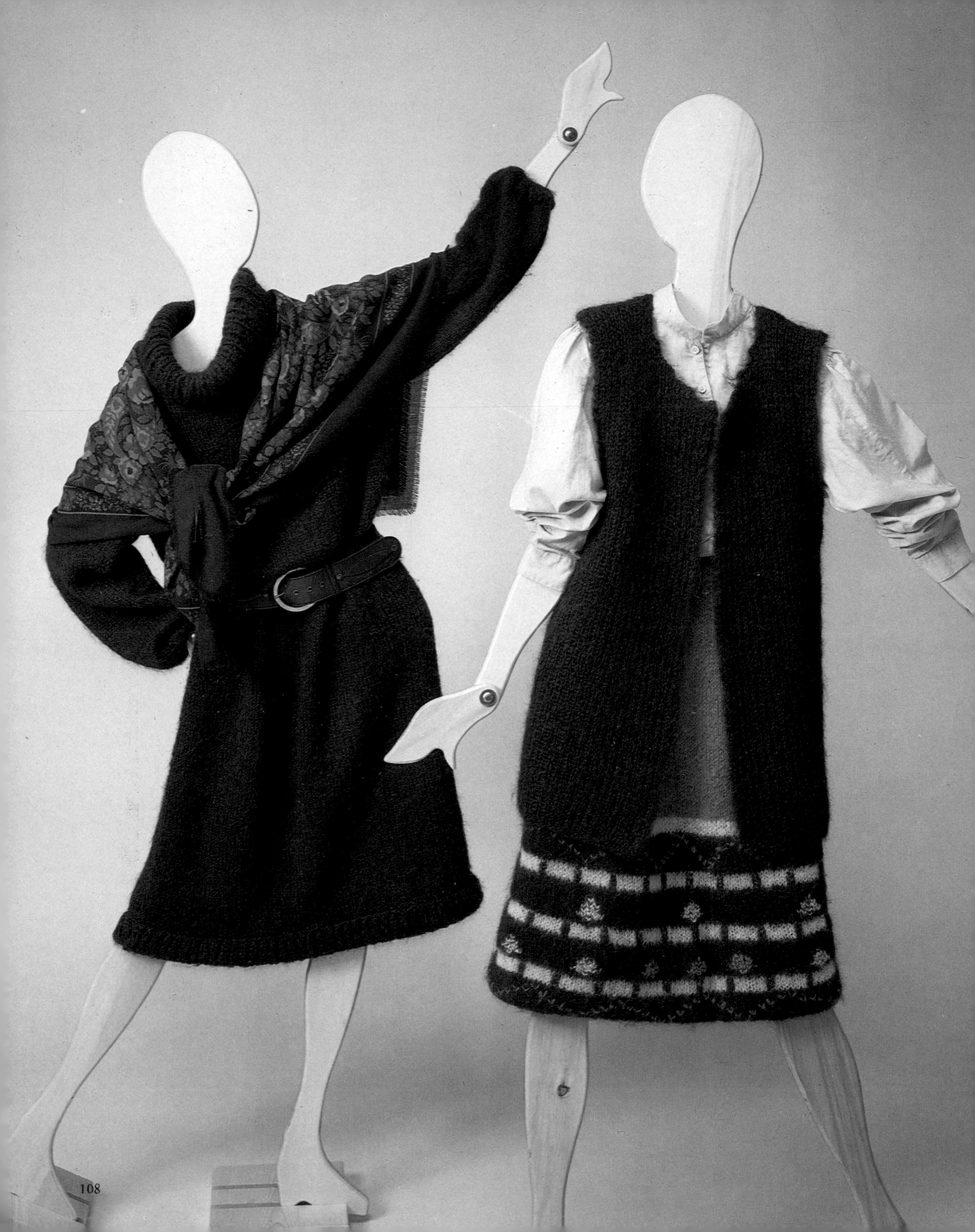

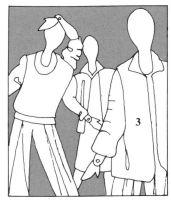

The garments illustrated in colour on p. 107.

Beginning of armhole shaping →

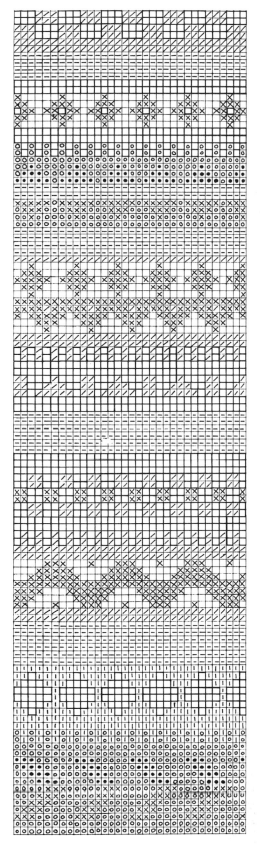

Chart for blue Jacquard jacket

☐ light blue background
✕ blue silk
╱ dark blue
○ airforce blue
⬤ electric blue
⎮ deep blue
— garter stitch, changing colours

1 stitch at armhole edge. Finish the chart as for back and bind off shoulder stitches.

The other side is worked in the same way, reversing shapings.

● *Sleeves:* Cast on 35(40–45) stitches with orange wool and work 8cm(3″) in garter stitch, changing colour every 2 rows and using all 5 colours. Continue in stockinette stitch and Jacquard, following the chart and increasing 1 stitch at each end of every sixth row. When armhole shaping row indicated on chart is reached, bind off 3 stitches, then 2 stitches, then 1 stitch on each side. Continue, decreasing 1 stitch at each end of every row until chart has been worked through.

● *To make up:* Matching pattern, join side seams and shoulder seams. Join sleeve seams and insert sleeves. Using the crochet hook pick up stitches (see p. 42) along front edges, V-neck and back of neck beginning from lower righthand edge. Work 4cm(1½″) in garter stitch, changing colour every 2 rows and using all 5 colours.

Blue Jacquard jacket (3)
Illustrated in colour on p. 107

Standard ★★★
Tension: 19 stitches and 20 rows to 10cm(4″)
Size: Women's size 38. The figures in brackets refer to sizes 36 and 34.
Materials: 500g(450g–400g)/18oz(16oz–14oz) mohair, in 5 shades of blue
50g(2oz) blue silk
1 pair needles size 3.5mm(#4)
1 crochet hook size 3.5mm(#E)
3 blue buttons
Stitches used: Garter stitch (see p. 57). Jacquard knitting (see pp. 52-3).

Method
● *Back:* Cast on 90(85–80) stitches and work 18 rows in garter stitch, changing colour every 2 rows and using all 6 yarns.

Continue in Jacquard, following the chart until row where armhole shaping is indicated is reached; shape armholes by binding off 5 stitches on each side.

Continue until the whole chart has been worked through. Bind off.

● *Fronts:* Cast on 43(40–38) stitches and work 18 rows in garter stitch, changing colour every 2 rows and using all 6 yarns.

Continue in Jacquard following the chart until armhole shaping is indicated; work armhole shaping as for back.

Work 15cm(6") following chart, then shape neck, binding off 8 stitches, then 1 stitch 5 times at neck edge. When front measures same as back, bind off. Work other side in the same way, reversing shapings.

● *Sleeves:* Cast on 50(45–40) stitches and work 18 rows in garter stitch, changing colour every 2 rows and using all 6 yarns.

Continue in stockinette stitch and Jacquard, following chart until armhole shaping is reached; on each side bind off 5 stitches, then 1 stitch 14(13–12) times. Bind off remaining stitches.

● *To make up:* Join side, shoulder and sleeve seams. Insert sleeves.

Using the crochet hook pick up stitches (see p. 42) along front edges and work 12 rows in garter stitch, changing colour every 2 rows and using all 6 yarns. On the right-hand border work 3 buttonholes over 2 stitches (see p. 45), the first 24cm(9½") from lower edge and the other two at 15cm(6") intervals.

Pick up the stitches around neck edge and work 12 rows in garter stitch, changing colour every 2 rows and using all 6 yarns.

Brown cowl-neck dress (1)
Illustrated in colour on p. 108

Standard: ★★
Tension: 16 stitches and 18 rows to 10cm(4")
Size: One size, to fit bust 34, 36 and 38.
Materials: 700g(24oz) dark brown alpaca wool
1 pair needles size 5mm(#8)

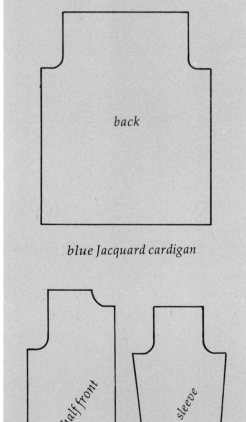

blue Jacquard cardigan

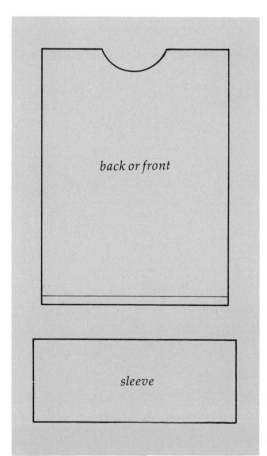

1 set of 4 needles size 5mm(#8)
1 crochet hook size 5mm(#H)
Lining material
Elastic 1.5cm(¾″) wide
Stitches used: Stockinette stitch (see p. 57). Single rib (see p. 57).

Method
● *Back:* Cast on 90 stitches and work 4cm(1½″) in single rib.

Change to stockinette stitch and work 90cm(35½″), then bind off the 30 central stitches. Working each side separately, at shoulder edge bind off 10 stitches 3 times.
● *Front:* Work the same as back.
● *Sleeves:* Cast on 50 stitches and work a simple hem (see p. 44) 2cm(¾″) deep. Continue in stockinette stitch for 40cm(16″). Bind off.
● *To make up:* Beginning at lower edge join side seams for 40cm(16″), leave a 10cm(4″) gap, then continue seam leaving a gap for the sleeves. Join shoulders and sleeve seams and insert sleeves.

Using the crochet hook pick up the stitches (see p. 42) around the neck and transfer the stitches to the set of four needles. Work 18cm(7″) in single rib, then bind off invisibly (see p. 31).

With the lining material make 2 pocket linings measuring 11cm × 11cm(4¼″ × 4¼″); insert these into the gaps left in the side seams and slip-stitch into place.

Thread the elastic through the wrist hems, gather, and fasten elastic.

The garments illustrated in colour on p. 108.

Brown alpaca sweater (2)
Illustrated in colour on p. 108

Standard: ★
Tension: 16 stitches and 18 rows to 10cm(4″)
Size: One size, to fit bust 34, 36 and 38.
Materials: 280g(10oz) dark brown alpaca wool
1 pair needles size 5mm(#8)
Stitches used: Single rib (see p. 57).

Method:
● *Back:* Cast on 70 stitches and work in single rib for 45cm(17¾″). Shape armholes by binding off 3 stitches on each side. Continue in single rib for 23cm(9″). Bind off.

● *Fronts:* Cast on 35 stitches and work 45cm(17¾″) in single rib. Shape armhole by binding off 3 stitches, then 1 stitch. Continue in single rib for 15cm(6″) then shape neck: at neck edge bind off 4 stitches, then 2 stitches, then 1 stitch twice. Continue in single rib until front measures same as back. Bind off.
● *To make up:* Stitch side and shoulder seams.

Brown Jacquard skirt (3)
Illustrated in colour on p. 108

Standard: ★★★
Tension: 13 stitches and 18 rows to 10cm(4″)
Size: Women's size 36. The figures in brackets refer to sizes 34 and 38.
Materials: 230(200–260g)/8oz(7oz–9oz) beige alpaca wool
120(100–140g)/4oz(3½oz–4½oz) brown alpaca wool
50g(2oz) white alpaca wool
1 pair needles size 5mm(#8)
Waist elastic 2.5cm(1″) wide
Zipper
Stitches used: Single rib (see p. 57). Stockinette stitch (see p. 57). Jacquard knitting (see pp. 52-3).

Method
● The skirt is worked in 2 identical halves starting from the waist.

Cast on 62(58–66) stitches using beige wool and work 16(14–18)cm/6¼(5½–7)″ in single rib.

113

Chart for the brown Jacquard skirt. Follow the chart from TOP to BOTTOM.

☐ brown background
○ white
V Swiss darning, over 2 stitches in beige
● Swiss darning in beige
Ø Swiss darning in white

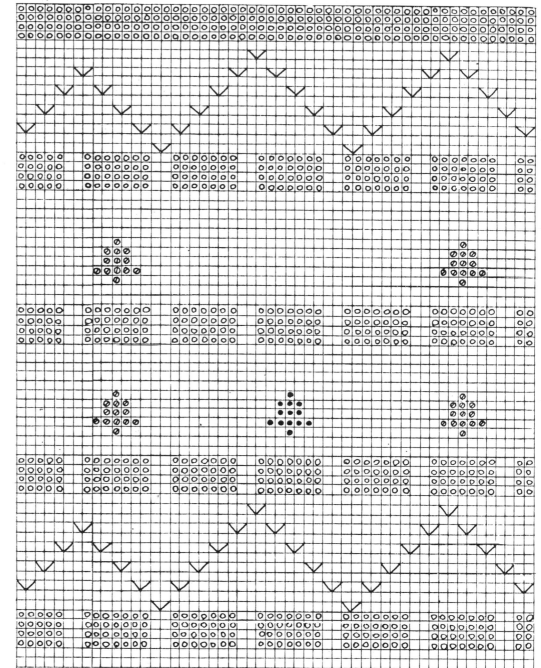

Continue in stockinette stitch for 30(27–33)cm/12(10½–13)″, gradually increasing 1 stitch at each end of every row until there are 98 (91–105) stitches. Work the Jacquard pattern in stockinette stitch, following the chart from top to bottom. When the chart has been worked through, work 1 row in purl on right side of work, then 4cm(1½″) in stockinette stitch.

● *To make up:* Join side seams, leaving an opening 20cm(8″) long in the left-hand seam for zipper.

Fold 3cm(1¼″) of upper edge over and slip-stitch; attach elastic using herringbone stitch as described on p. 146.

Turn up lower hem along purl row and slip-stitch. Insert zipper.

Using swiss darning (see p. 140) embroider the motif shown on the chart.

The garments illustrated in colour on p. 109.

Sage green coat (1)
Illustrated in colour on p. 109

Standard: ★★
Tension: 11 stitches and 19 rows to 10cm(4″)
Size: To fit women's size 38. The figures in brackets refer to sizes 36 and 40.
Materials: 1,200g (1,000g–1,400g) /43oz (36oz–48oz) sage green sport yarn
1 pair needles size 6mm(#10)
3 green buttons
It is advisable to line the coat.
Stitches used: Stockinette stitch (see p. 57). Simple cable stitch (see p. 62). Garter stitch (see p. 57).

Method

● *Back:* Cast on 82(78–86) stitches and work a simple hem (see p. 44) 4cm(1½″)wide. Continue in stockinette stitch for 20cm(8″); decreasing 1 stitch at each end of every twelfth row, work another 56(52–60)cm/22(20½–23½)″.

To shape armholes bind off 3 stitches at each side on alternate rows 3 times. Continue for 15(14–16)cm/6(5½–6¼)″. Shape shoulders: bind off 4 stitches at each side on alternate rows 3 times. Bind off remaining stitches for back of neck.

● *Fronts:* Cast on 50(48–52) stitches and work a simple hem (see p. 44) 4cm(1½″) deep. Continue in stockinette stitch working the 12 front edge stitches in simple cable as follows: 2 stitches in garter stitch, 8 stitches in cable, 2 stitches in garter stitch. When 20cm(8″) have been worked decrease 1 stitch on left-hand edge 6 times at regular intervals.

When 30(27–33)cm/11¾ (10½–13)″ have been worked make a horizontal pocket (see p. 46) 15cm(6″) wide.

Work another 26cm(10″), then shape armhole at side edge; bind off 3 stitches on alternate rows 3 times.

Work 12cm(4¾″) then shape neck: bind off 20 stitches, then 2 stitches at neck edge 3 times. Bind off shoulder stitches as for back.

Work the other side in the same way, reversing shapings.
● *Sleeves:* Cast on 36(34–38) stitches and work a simple hem (see p. 44) 4cm(1½″) deep. Continue in stockinette stitch for 43(42–44)cm/17(16½–17¼)″ increasing 1 stitch at each end of every fourth row.

Shape top by binding off 2 stitches at each side 4 times, then 1 stitch 6 times. Bind off.
● *To make up:* Join side seams and shoulder seams. Join sleeve seams and insert sleeves.

To finish neck, cast on 12 stitches and

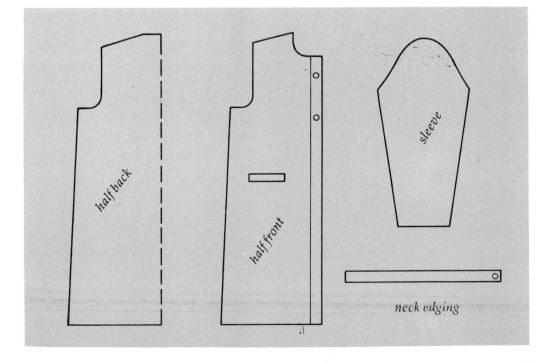

half back

half front

sleeve

neck edging

work 68cm(27") in simple cable as described for front border. Bind off.

Stitch this border around neck edge, allowing 5cm(2") to project at right front edge. Make 2 buttonholes on front border by cutting 1 stitch and finishing buttonhole with buttonhole stitch; make one buttonhole 10cm(4") below neck shaping, the second 16cm(6¼") below the first. A third buttonhole should be made in the projecting end of the neck border, 1 cm(½") from the end. Sew on the 3 buttons to match buttonholes.

Brown coat (2)
Illustrated in colour on p. 109

Standard: ★★
Tension: 10 stitches and 20 rows to 10cm(4")
Size: Women's size 36. The figures in brackets refer to sizes 34 and 38.
Materials: 1,300g (1,200g–1,400g)/46oz (44oz–48oz) brown sport yarn
1 pair needles size 7mm(#10½)
Stitches used: Stockinette stitch (see p. 57). Single rib (see p. 57). Seed stitch (see p. 59).

Method
• *Back:* Cast on 68(64–72) stitches and work in seed stitch for 79(77–81)cm/ 31(30¼–32)". Shape armholes by binding off 2 stitches at each end on alternate rows 3 times. Continue for 18(17–19)cm/ 7(6¾–7½)" in seed stitch but work the first 6 stitches and the last 6 stitches in stockinette stitch. Bind off.
• *Fronts:* Cast on 40(38–42) stitches and work in single rib on the first 8 stitches in seed stitch on the remainder. Work 45(43–47)cm/17¾(17–18½)" then make a vertical inset pocket (see p. 46) 14cm(5½") long. Continue for 10cm(4") then shape armhole: bind off 2 stitches at side edge on alternate rows 3 times. Continue for 16(15–17)cm/6¼ (6–6¾)", working the first 8 stitches for front band in single rib, the central stitches in seed stitch and the last 6 stitches in stockinette stitch.

To shape neck bind off 12 stitches at neck edge, then 2 stitches on alternate rows 4 times. Bind off remaining shoulder stitches.

Work the other front in the same way, reversing shapings.
• *Sleeves:* Cast on 30(28–32) stitches and work 41(39–43)cm/16(15½–17)" in seed stitch, inceasing 1 stitch at each end of every sixth row. Shape top by binding off 3 stitches, then 1 stitch 10(9–11) times at both sides. Bind off.

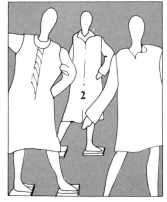

The garments illustrated in colour on p. 109.

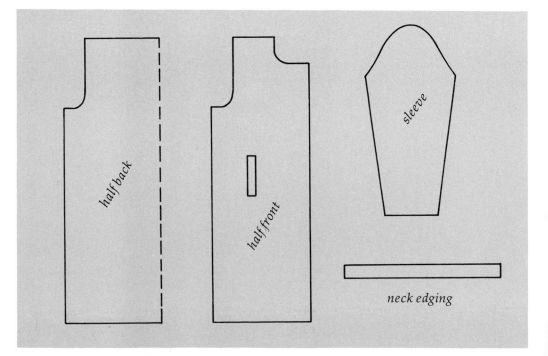

half back

half front

sleeve

neck edging

- *To make up:* Join side seams and shoulder seams; join sleeve seams and insert sleeves.

To finish neck, cast on 60 stitches and work 4cm(1½") in seed stitch; working the first and last 8 stitches of every row in single rib. Work 6cm(2¼") in single rib over all the stitches. Bind off.

Stitch this strip to neck edge.

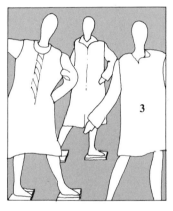

The garments illustrated in colour on p. 109.

Double-face coat (3)
Illustrated in colour on p. 109

Standard ★★★
Tension: 9 stitches and 11 rows to 10cm(4")
Size: Women's size 36. The figures in brackets refer to sizes 34 and 38.
Materials: 600g(500g–700g)/20oz(16oz–24oz) brown alpaca wool
600g(500g–700g)/20oz(16oz–24oz) grey alpaca wool
Double pointed needles size 9mm(#15)
2 buttons, 1 grey, 1 brown
Lining material
Stitches used: Double-face knitting (see pp. 53-4).

Method
- *Back:* Using brown wool cast on 45(42–48) stitches and work in double-face knitting with both colours in stockinette stitch for 58(56–60)cm/23(22–23½)". Shape armholes by binding off 2 stitches on alternate rows 3 times.

Continue in double-face knitting, working 21(20–22)cm/8¼(8–8¾)", then shape shoulders by binding off 4 stitches on alternate rows twice. Bind off remaining stitches.
- *Fronts:* Using brown wool cast on 32(30–28) stitches and work in double-face knitting with both colours in stockinette stitch for 58(56–60)cm/23(22–23½)". Shape armhole by binding off 2 stitches at armhole edge 3 times. Work 6cm(2¼") then make a horizontal

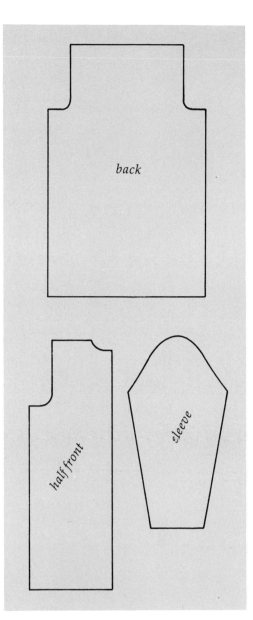

back

half front

sleeve

buttonhole (see p. 45) over 3 stitches.

Work 2 rows, then shape neck: bind off 10 stiches, then 2 stitches on alternate rows 3 times. When front measures same as back bind off shoulder stitches over 2 rows.

The other front is worked in the same way, reversing shapings.
- *Sleeves:* Using brown wool cast on 26(24–28) stitches and work in double-face knitting with both colours in stockinette stitch for 42(41–43)cm/16½(16–17)". Shape top by binding off 2 stitches on alternate rows twice, then 1 stitch on alternate rows 6 times. Bind off.

• *To make up:* Join side seams, leaving a 18cm(7″) gap for pocket 21cm(8¼″) from lower edge. Join shoulder seams and sleeve seams; insert sleeves.

Sew on buttons opposite buttonholes, one on the outside and one on the inside.

Make pocket linings from the lining material and insert them into the gaps in side seams; stitch edges.

With tiny back-stitches (see p. 143) sew around the neck and down both fronts; the stitching should be 2cm(¾″) from neck edge and ½cm(¼″) from front edge.

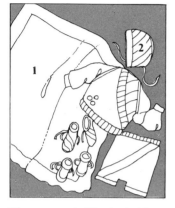

The garments illustrated in colour on p. 110.

Baby's layette: blanket (1)
Illustrated in colour on p. 110

Standard: ★
Tension: 17 stitches and 22 rows to 10cm(4″)
Size: The blanket measures 60cm × 75cm(23½″ × 29½″) and is suitable for either a pram or a cot.
Materials: 140g(5oz) 4-ply sport yarn in cream
60g(2½oz) 4-ply sport yarn in yellow
1 pair needles size 5mm(#8)
1 crochet hook size 5mm(#H)
Stitches used: Garter stitch (see p. 57). Diagonal openwork pattern (see p. 78). Shrimp stitch border (see p. 43).

Method
• Cast on 107 stitches using yellow wool and work 5cm(2″) in garter stitch. Change to cream wool and diagonal openwork stitch, continuing to work the first and last stitches of every row in garter stitch. Work 50cm(19¾″), then change to garter stitch and yellow wool and work 5cm(2″).

Using the crochet hook and yellow wool pick up the stitches (see p. 42) along the short sides of the blanket and work 5cm(2″) in garter stitch.

Using yellow wool and cream wool together work a row of crocheted shrimp stitch border around the edge of the blanket.

Baby's layette: bonnet (2)
Illustrated in colour on p. 110

Standard: ★★
Tension: 34 stitches and 48 rows to 10cm(4″)

Size: To fit size up to 1 month. The figures in brackets refer to the sizes for 3 months and 6 months.
Materials: 10g (15g–20g) /½oz (½oz–1oz) yellow 3-ply baby wool
1 pair needles size 2.5mm(#0)
1 crochet hook size 2.5mm(#3)
Yellow ribbon
1 yellow silk flower
Stitches used: Stockinette stitch (see p. 57). Garter stitch (see p. 57)

Method: The bonnet is knitted in one piece, beginning at the front border.

Cast on 95(103–111) stitches and work 10 rows in garter stitch. Continue in stockinette stitch, working an eyelet every 6 stitches on knit rows as follows: yrn, slip 1, k.1, psso. Move the eyelet one stitch to the left on every knit row, thus the second knit row will begin k.7, the third k.8 and so on.

Work 4cm(1½″) then begin another line of eyelets to the right of the first line as follows: *k.6, yrn, slip.1, k.1, psso*. Move this line of eyelets one stitch to the

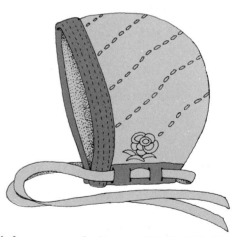

left on every knit row. Work 4(6–8)cm/1½(2¼–3)″.

Leaving 27 stitches on either side on spare needles, work on the 41(49–57) central stitches in stockinette stitch. On each row pick up one of the stitches from each spare needle, passing the last of the central stitches over the first of the side stitches on a knit row, and knitting together the last of the central stitches and the first of the side stitches on a purl row.

At the same time work the 5 central stitches as follows: k.1, slip.1, psso, k.1, k.2 tog (thus decreasing 2 stitches). Repeat until 5 stitches are left; bind off.

● *To make up:* Using the crochet hook pick up the stitches (see p. 42) around base of bonnet and work 2 rows in garter stitch.

Work a row of eyelets for the ribbon as follows: k.2, *yrn, k.2 tog, k.4*, k.2. Continue in garter stitch for 5 rows. Bind off.

Thread the ribbon through the holes and stitch the yellow silk flower on the lower left-hand corner, as illustrated.

The garments illustrated in colour on p. 110.

Baby's layette: sweater (3)
Illustrated in colour on p. 110.

Standard: ★★★
Tension: 34 stitches and 48 rows to 10cm(4″)

Size: The jacket is for up to 1 month. The figures in brackets refer to the sizes for 3 months and 6 months.

Materials: 40g(60g–80g)/1½oz(2½oz–3oz) yellow 3-ply baby wool
1 pair needles size 2.5mm(#1)
3 yellow silk flowers
2 small yellow buttons

Stitches used: Single rib (see p. 57). Stockinette stitch (see p. 57). Garter stitch (see p. 57).

Method

● *Back:* Cast on 65(73–81) stitches using one of the invisible methods of casting on described on pp. 30-1. Work 3 rows in k.1 slip 1 rib. Continue in single rib for 2.5cm(1″) then work 1 knit row, increasing 1 stitch every 8(9–10) stitches, thus increasing 8 times. Continue in stockinette stitch, working the first 2 stitches and the last 2 stitches in garter stitch, for 9(11–13)cm/3½(4–5)″.

Decrease for raglan armholes as follows: on every knit row k.2, slip 1, k.1, psso, work to last 4 stitches, k.2 tog, k.2.

Continue to decrease on right side of work until 19(21–23) stitches remain. Bind off.

● *Right front:* Cast on 65(73–81) stitches as on back; work 3 rows in k.1 slip 1 rib. Continue in single rib for 2.5cm(1″), then work 1 knit row increasing 1 stitch every 8(9–10) stitches, thus increasing 8 times. Work 1 purl row, working the first

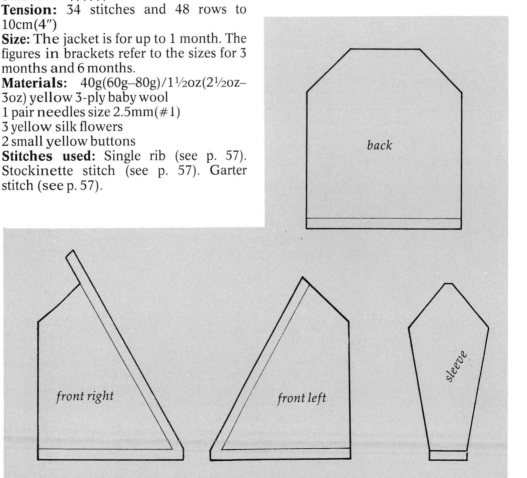

back

front right

front left

sleeve

2 and last 6 stitches in garter stitch.

Now begin the transverse eyelet pattern and the shaping of the front crossover, working knit rows as follows: k.6, slip 1, k.1, psso (this is the decrease for the crossover shaping), k.10, yarn around needle, slip 1, k.1, psso, k.10, yarn around needle, slip 1, k.1, psso, knit to end. Purl return rows, working first 2 and last 6 stitches in garter stitch. To obtain oblique parallel lines of eyelets, on each knit row move the pattern 1 stitch to the left thus: k.6, slip 1, k.1, psso (crossover shaping), k.11 (on subsequent rows k.12, 13, 14, etc.), yarn around needle, slip 1, k.1, psso, k.10, yarn around needle, slip 1, k.1, psso, knit to end of row.

When 9(11–13)cm/3½(4–5)" have been worked begin raglan shaping; k.2 tog on side opposite crossover before final 2 stitches in garter stitch. Continue decreasing on knit rows until armhole shaping measures same as back armhole shaping. Bind off all stitches except the 6 garter stitches. Continue on these until the garter stitch border is the same length as the back neck shaping.

● *Left front:* Cast on 65(73–81) stitches as on back; work 3 rows in k.1 slip 1 rib. Continue in single rib for 2.5cm(1"), then work 1 knit row increasing 1 stitch every 8(9–10) stitches, thus increasing 8 times.

On following purl row begin working transverse eyelet pattern and shaping crossover. The eyelet pattern is worked as follows: k.6 (garter stitch border), p.2 tog (crossover shaping), p.10, yarn around needle, p.2 tog, p.10, yarn around needle, p.2 tog, purl to last 2 stitches, k.2. To obtain oblique parallel lines of eyelets, on following purl rows increase first 10 purl stitches by 1 each time as follows: k.6 (garter stitch border), p.2 tog (crossover shaping), p.11 (on subsequent rows p.12, 13, 14 etc.), yarn around needle, p.2 tog, p.10, yarn around needle, p.2 tog, purl to last 2 stitches, k.2.

When 9(11–13)cm/3½(4¼–5)" have been worked, begin armhole shaping on side opposite crossover shaping. On knit rows decrease 1 stitch as follows: knit to last 4 stitches, k.1, slip 1, psso, k.2.

Continue decreasing until front measures same as back from armhole. Bind off.

● *Sleeves:* Cast on 40(45–50) stitches as on back: work 3 rows in k.1 slip rib. Continue in single rib for 3cm(1¼") then work 1 knit row, increasing every 8(9–10) stitches, thus increasing 5 times. Continue in stockinette stitch, working the first and last 2 stitches in garter stitch, for 15(17–19)cm/6(6¾–7½)" and increasing 1 stitch at each end of the row, between the 2 garter stitches, every 8 rows.

Shape raglan top by working every knit row as follows: k.2, slip 1, k.1, psso, knit to last 4 stitches, k.2 tog, k.2. When raglan measures same as back raglan, bind off.

● *To make up:* Join side seams and sleeve seams; insert sleeves.

Pin extension of border knitted on right front around neck and stitch, then stitch it to left front border.

Sew buttons to left front just above ribbing and make two buttonholes on right front to correspond; for each buttonhole cut 1 stitch and work around it in buttonhole stitch (see p. 145).

Stitch the silk flowers carefully to right front.

Baby's layette: mittens (4)
Illustrated in colour on p. 110

Standard: ★★

Tension: 34 stitches and 48 rows to 10cm(4")

Size: The mittens are for up to 1 month. The figures in brackets refer to sizes for 3 months and 6 months.

Materials: 10g (20g–30g) /½oz (1oz–1½oz) yellow 3-ply baby wool
1 pair needles size 2.5mm(#1)
Yellow ribbon

Stitches used: Single rib (see p. 57). Diagonal openwork pattern (see p. 78). Stockinette stitch (see p. 57).

Method
● The mittens are worked in one piece, beginning at the wrist.

Cast on 42(46–50) stitches using one of the invisible methods of casting on (see pp. 30-1) and work 2 rows in k.1 slip 1 rib.

Continue in single rib for 3(3.5–4)cm/ 1¼(1½–1¾)″, then work a row of eyelets for the ribbon as follows: *k.2 tog, yarn around needle*, repeat to end of row. Change to diagonal openwork stitch on first 20 stitches (this will be the back of the mitten) and stockinette stitch on the remaining stitches (this will be the palm of the mitten); work 4(5–5.5)cm/1½(2– 2¼)″, then begin decreasing for top of mitten, working in stockinette stitch as follows:

On knit rows only *k.4, k.2 tog* to end of row. Repeat until 7 stitches remain. Bind off.

● *To make up:* Join sides of mittens on wrong side with small, invisible stitches. Stitch across tops, also on wrong side.

Turn mittens right-side out and, using a bodkin or yarn needle, thread yellow ribbon through eyelets.

The garments illustrated in colour on p. 110.

Baby's layette: bootees (5)
Illustrated in colour on p. 110

Standard: ★★
Tension: 34 stitches and 48 rows to 10cm(4″)
Size: The bootees are for up to 1 month. The figures in brackets refer to sizes for 3 months and 6 months.
Materials: 10(15g–20g)/½oz(½oz–1oz) yellow 3-ply baby wool
1 pair needles size 2.5mm(#1)
Yellow ribbon
Stitches used: Stockinette stitch (see p. 57). Single rib (see p. 57).

Method
The bootees are worked in one piece beginning at the sole of the foot.

Cast on 38(44–50) stitches and work 2 rows in stockinette stitch. Continue in stockinette stitch increasing (on knit rows only) 1 stitch after the first stitch, 1 stitch before the last stitch, and 1 stitch on either side of the 2 central stitches (thus increasing 4 stitches on every knit row) until there are 58(64–70) stitches.

With right side of work facing, work as follows: *1 row purl, 1 row knit, 1 row purl*. Repeat from * to * 4 times, thus alternating 3 rows of stockinette stitch and reversed stockinette stitch.

These 15 rows give a furrowed effect which is very elastic; the number of rows need not be altered for the different sizes.

Continue in stockinette stitch working on the 10 central stitches only. Transfer the side stitches to spare needles and add 1 stitch from alternate spare needles to the central stitches at the beginning of each row. When 9(13–17) stitches have been added. the top of the foot is complete; 18(26–34) rows will have been worked in stockinette stitch. Knit 1 row, then work eyelets for ribbon as follows: *p.2 tog, yarn around needle*, repeat to end of row.

Change to single rib and work 5(6– 7)cm/2(2¼–2¾)″. Bind off.
● *To make up:* Join the sole and the back seam. Thread ribbon through eyelets.

Baby's layette: short trousers (6)
Illustrated in colour on p. 110

Standard: ★★
Tension: 34 stitches and 48 rows to 10cm(4″)
Size: To fit up to 1 month. The figures in brackets refer to the sizes for 3 months and 6 months.
Materials: 40g (50g–60g) /1½oz (2oz–2½oz) yellow 3-ply baby wool
1 pair needles size 2.5mm(#1)
Yellow ribbon
Stitches used: Single rib (see p. 57). Stockinette stitch (see p. 57). Garter stitch (see p. 57).

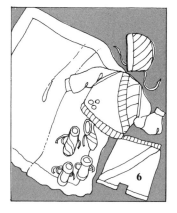

The garments illustrated in colour on p. 110.

Method
● *Back:* Cast on 64(70–76) stitches using one of the invisible methods of casting on described on pp. 30-1. Work 4 rows in k.1 slip 1 rib. Continue in single rib for 1(1.5–2)cm/½(¾–1)″. Work the eyelets for the ribbon in the next row as follows: *k.3, k.2 tog, yarn around needle*, k.3. Continue in stockinette stitch for 14(16–18)cm/5½(6¼–7)″, then work the gusset as follows: increase on each side of the 2 central stitches on every knit row until 14(18–22) stitches have been increased.

Bind off the gusset stitches and, continuing in stockinette stitch, work both legs separately. Work 2(4–6)cm/¾(1½–2¼)″ in stockinette stitch. Change to garter stitch and work 8 rows. Bind off.
● *Front:* Cast on 64(70–76) stitches as on back. Work 4 rows in k.1 slip 1 rib. Continue in single rib for 1(1.5–2)cm/½(¾–1)″. Work a row of eyelets for the ribbon as follows: *k.3, k.2 tog, yarn around needle*, k.3.

Work 1 purl row, 1 knit row, then begin working diagonal openwork motif as follows: p.10, yarn around needle, p.2 tog, p.10, yarn around needle, p.2 tog, purl to end. Knit following row and all right side rows. On following purl rows, to obtain oblique parallel lines, move the eyelets 1 stitch along each time: i.e. the second purl row will begin p.11, the third will begin p.12, the fourth p.13 etc. Ten stitches always remain between the two lines of eyelet pattern.

When 14(16–18)cm/5½(6¼–7)″ have been worked in pattern begin the gusset shaping: increase on either side of the 2 central stitches 1 stitch on every knit row until 14(18–22) stitches have been increased. Bind off gusset stitches and continue on both sides separately. Work 1 leg in stockinette stitch and the other continuing the openwork pattern; work 2(4–6)cm/¾(1½–2¼)″. Change to garter stitch and work 8 rows. Bind off.
● *To make up:* Join side seams, gusset and inside leg seams. Thread yellow ribbon through eyelets.

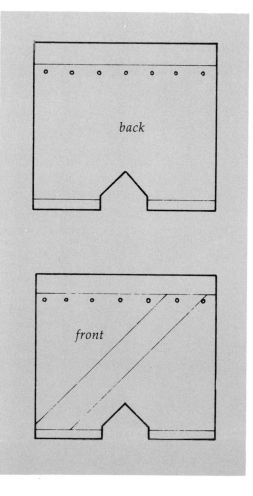

Pink jacket (1)

Illustrated in colour on p. 127

Standard ★★

Tension: 30 stitches and 33 rows to 10cm(4″)

Size: The jacket is for children aged 1-2 years. The figures in brackets refer to the size for 2-3 year olds.

Materials: 260g (300g) /10oz (10½oz) pink mohair

1 pair needles size 2.5mm(#1)

3 white buttons

Stitches used: Stockinette stitch (see p. 57). Double rib (see p. 58).

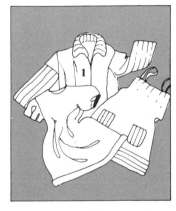

The garments illustrated in colour on p. 127.

Method

● *Back:* Cast on 98(104) stitches and work 16cm(6¼″) in stockinette stitch.

Change to double rib and work 18(21)cm/7(8¼)″ beginning on the wrong side of work. Change to reverse stockinette stitch, beginning with a purl row on right side of work and shape armholes by binding off on each side 2 stitches 4 times.

Work 7(8)cm/2¾(3″), then bind off for shoulders 4 stitches on each side 7 times. Bind off remaining stitches.

● *Fronts:* Cast on 48 stitches and work 16cm(6¼″) in stockinette stitch. Change to double rib and work 18(21)cm/7(8¼)″ beginning on wrong side of work.

Change to reverse stockinette stitch, beginning with a purl row on right side of

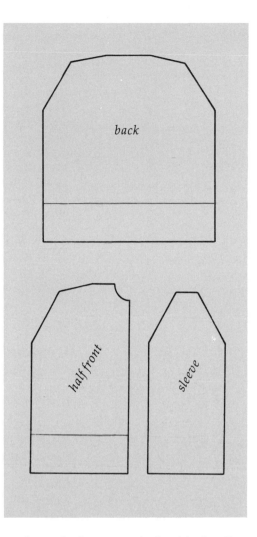

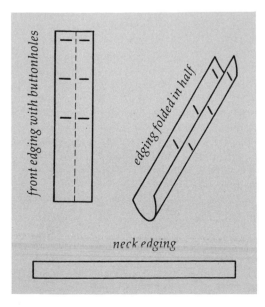

work and shape armhole: bind off 2 stitches 4 times. Work 4cm(1½″), then shape neck on side opposite armhole: at neck edge bind off 2 stitches 7 times. Bind off shoulder stitches.

● *Sleeves:* Cast on 68(74) stitches and work 20(24)cm/8(9½)″ in double rib.

With wrong side of work facing work 1 knit row, knitting together all the pairs of purl stitches of the double rib. Continue in reverse stockinette stitch, shaping armhole top by decreasing 1 stitch on either side of work on every row 8 times. Bind off.

● *To make up:* Join side and shoulder seams. Join sleeve seams and insert sleeves.

For collar, cast on 92 stitches and work 9cm(3½″) in double rib: a rectangle will be obtained.

The front borders are made of 2 strips

worked as follows: cast on 110(120) stitches and work 6cm(2¼") in reverse stockinette stitch. Bind off.

On one of the strips work 3 horizontal buttonholes (see p. 45) over 2 stitches, beginning 1.5cm(½") from the start of the row – on the fifth and sixth stitches. The other 2 buttonholes should be 6cm(2¼") apart.

Three more buttonholes should be worked 3cm(1¼") from the first 3 and in exactly the same position.

Fold strips in half lengthwise, matching buttonholes. Stitch to fronts and work around buttonholes in blanket stitch (see p. 145). Stitch collar to neck edge. Sew on buttons.

Fold lower edge of stockinette stitch and slip-stitch neatly.

Grey and blue dress (2)
Illustrated in colour on p. 127

Standard ★★
Tension: 25 stitches and 28 rows to 10cm(4")
Size: To fit babies of 8-10 months. The figures in brackets refer to sizes for 2 and 3 years.
Materials: 60g(80g–100g)/2½oz(3oz–3½oz) grey kid mohair
20g(30g–40g)/½oz(1oz–1½oz) blue silk
1 pair needles size 3mm(#3)
Crochet hook size 3(#C)
4 blue buttons
Stitches used: Stockinette stitch (see p. 57). Garter stitch (see p. 57).

Method
● *Back and Front:* Worked in one piece. Cast on 112(124–136) stitches in wool and work a simple hem (see p. 44) 1.5cm(½") deep. Continue in stockinette stitch for 28(30–32)cm/11(11¾–12½"), then join in silk and work in silk and wool as follows to gather bodice:
Rows 1 and 2: knit, using silk.
Rows 3, 5 and 7: using wool, k.1 *slip 2 purlwise with wool back, k.4*, slip 2 purlwise, k.1.
Rows 4, 6 and 8: using wool, p.1, *slip 2 purlwise with wool forward, p.4*, p.1.
Rows 9 and 10: knit, using silk.
Rows 11, 13 and 15: using wool, k.4, *slip

2 purlwise with wool back, k.4*, slip 2, k.4.
Rows 12, 14 and 16: using wool, p.4, *slip 2 purlwise with wool forward, p.4* slip 2, p.4.
Repeat these 16 rows for 7(9–11)cm/ 2¾(3½–4¼)". Continuing to work with

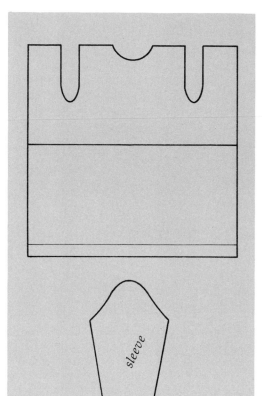

wool and silk in pattern as above, divide the work into three thus: work 25(28–31) stitches, bind off 6, work 50(56–62) stitches, bind off 6, work 25(28–31). The two sets of 25 stitches will form the left and right back; the group of 50 stitches will form the front. On the first and last group of stitches work 9(11–13)cm/ 3½(4¼–5)", then bind off. Work 7(10–12) cm/2¾(4–4¾)" on the 50 central stitches, then shape neck: bind off the 4(6–8) central stitches and work each side separately until front measures same as back. Bind off.
● *Sleeves:* Cast on 34(40–46) stitches and work 10 rows in pattern using wool

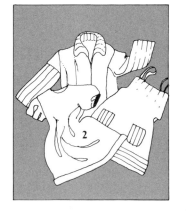

The garments illustrated in colour on p. 127.

and silk to gather work as described above for back and front. Continue in stockinette stitch in wool for 8(10–12) cm/3(4–4¾)″, increasing 1 stitch at each end of every sixth row. Shape top: bind off 3 stitches at each side, then decrease 1 stitch on every row; work 6(8–10)cm/2½(3–4)″. Bind off one third of the remaining stitches at the beginning of the next 3 rows to shape top.

● *To make up:* Join the back seam, leaving the bodice in silk and wool pattern open. Join shoulder seams and insert sleeves.

Using the crochet hook and silk, pick up the stitches (see p. 42) along each open edge of the back; work 3 rows in garter stitch. On one side make 3 baby clothes buttonholes (see p. 45).

Pick up the stitches around the neck, beginning from left back, across front then across right back. Work 4 rows in garter stitch. Bind off.

Sew on buttons to match buttonholes.

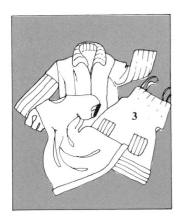

The garments illustrated in colour on p. 127.

Pinafore dress in yellow mohair (3)

Illustrated in colour on p. 127

Standard: ★

Tension: 26 stitches and 22 rows to 10cm(4″)

Size: To fit children of 3 years. The figures in brackets refer to sizes for 4 and 5 years.

Materials: 110g (130g–150g) /3¾oz (4¼oz–5oz) yellow mohair.

1 pair needles size 3.5mm(#4)

Stitches used: Stockinette stitch (see p. 57). Garter stitch (see p. 57). Double rib (see p. 58).

Method

● *Back:* Cast on 90(100–110) stitches and work a simple hem (see p. 44) 4cm(1½″) wide. The stitches to be turned under should be worked in stockinette stitch; the visible part should be worked in garter stitch.

Continue in garter stitch for 30(32–34)cm/12(12½–13½)″, decreasing 1 stitch at each side on alternate rows.

Change to double rib and work 6(8–10)cm/2¼(3–4)″ without further shaping. To shape armholes bind off 3 stitches on each side. Bind off.

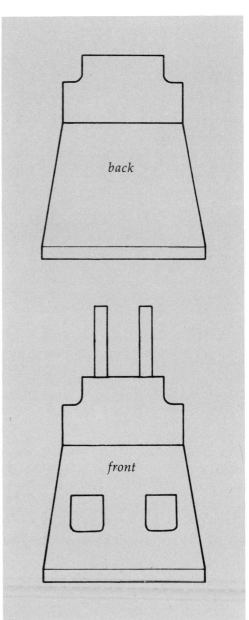

• *Front:* Work same as back to armhole shaping. When armholes have been shaped, leave 8 stitches at each end of row, and bind off central stitches. Work separately on each set of 8 stitches for shoulder straps, thus: using k.1 slip 1 rib (see p.30) work 12(14–16)cm/4¾(5½–6¼)".

• *Pockets:* Cast on 20 stitches and work 8cm(3") in double rib. Bind off. Work 2 pockets.

• *To make up:* Join side seams and attach shoulder straps to back. Sew on pockets.

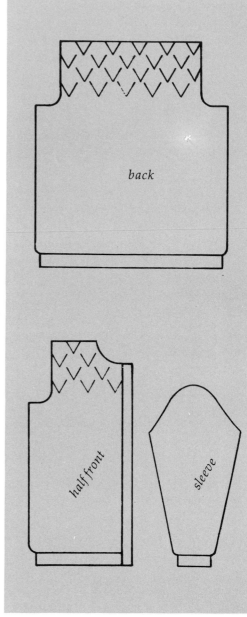

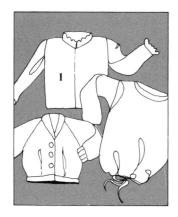

The garments illustrated in colour on p. 128.

Yellow cardigan: (1)
Illustrated in colour on p. 128

Standard: ★★
Tension: 24 stitches and 30 rows to 10cm(4")
Size: To fit babies of 8-10 months. The figures in brackets refer to sizes for 2 and 3 years.
Materials: 40g (50g–60g) /1½oz (2oz–2½oz) yellow Angora
A few grammes (or yards) silver lurex thread
1 pair needles size 3mm(#3)
1 crochet hook size 3mm(#C)
Stitches used: Garter stitch (see p. 57). Stockinette stitch (see p. 57). Crocheted bobble border (see p. 44). Swiss darning (see p. 140).

Method
• *Back:* With yellow Angora cast on 48(56–62) stitches and work 4cm(1½") in garter stitch. Change to stockinette stitch and work 20(23–25)cm/8(9–10)". Shape armholes by binding off 2 stitches at each end of row, then 1 stitch. Work 10(11–12)cm/4(4¼–4½)" in stockinette stitch. Bind off.

• *Fronts:* Cast on 24(28–31) stitches and work 4cm(1½") in garter stitch. Change to stockinette stitch and work 20(23–25)cm/8(9–10)" keeping the first 4 stitches at front edge in garter stitch.

Shape armholes by binding off 2 stitches then 1 stitch at side edge.

Continue in stockinette stitch for 3(4–5)cm/1¼(1½–2)", then shape neck. Bind off 4 stitches, then 2 stitches, then 1 stitch at front edge. Continue in stockinette stitch until front armhole measures same as back armhole. Bind off.

Work second front in the same way, reversing shapings.

• *Sleeves:* Cast on 28(35–42) stitches and work 4cm(1½") in garter stitch. Change to stockinette stitch and work 18(20–22)cm/7(8–9)", increasing 1 stitch at each end of every sixth row.

Shape top by binding off 2 stitches, then continue in stockinette stitch decreasing 1 stitch at each end of every row for 7(8–9)cm/2½(3–3½)″. Bind off one third of remaining stitches at the beginning of the next 3 rows.

● *To make up:* Join side seams and shoulder seams. Join sleeve seams and insert sleeves. Using a crochet hook and beginning at right front, pick up the stitches (see p. 42) around neck edge; work 4 rows in garter stitch. Bind off.

Work a crocheted bobble border (see p. 44) in Angora, working into first row of garter stitch edging along fronts and neck, and making two slip stitches into each knitted stitch.

Crochet a second bobble border along last row of garter stitch edgings, using lurex thread.

Finish the sleeves in the same way.

Using lurex thread and Swiss darning (see p. 140), embroider individual stitches on front and back as shown in the diagram.

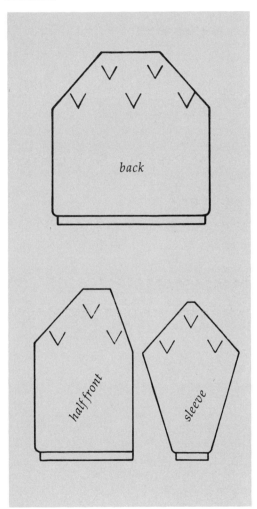

The garments illustrated in colour on the page opposite.

Mohair and silk cardigan (2)
Illustrated in colour on p. 128

Standard ★★
Tension: 28 stitches and 30 rows to 10cm(4″)

Size: The cardigan is to fit a 1-year-old baby. The figures in brackets refer to sizes for 2 and 3 years.

Materials: 30g(50g–70g)/1¼oz(2oz–2½oz) blue kid mohair

A few grammes (or yards) blue silk

A few grammes (or yards) silver lurex thread

1 pair needles size 3mm(#3)

1 crochet hook size 3(#C)

4 white buttons

Stitches used: Single rib (see p. 57). Garter stitch (see p. 57). Bouquet pattern (see p. 78). Swiss darning (see p. 104).

Method
● *Back:* Cast on 48(52–56) stitches and work 2cm(¾″) in single rib; change to bouquet pattern and work 20(23–25)cm/8(9–10)″. Shape raglan armholes, decreasing 1 stitch at each end of every knit row until armhole measures 9(10–11)cm/3½(4–4¼)″. Bind off remaining stitches.

● *Fronts:* Cast on 22(24–26) stitches and work 2cm(¾″) in single rib. Change to bouquet pattern and work 20(23–25)cm/8(9–10)″. Begin raglan shaping and neck shaping as follows. For raglan shaping, decrease 1 stitch at beginning of every knit row. For V-neck shaping bind off 1 stitch on every third purl row. When front raglan measures same as back raglan, bind off.

The other side is knitted in the same way, reversing shapings.

● *Sleeves:* Cast on 18(20–22) stitches and work 2cm(¾″) in single rib. Change to bouquet pattern and work 20(22–24)cm/8(8¾–9½)″, increasing 1 stitch at both ends of every tenth row. Shape raglan top, decreasing 1 stitch on every row until sleeve raglan measures same as back raglan. Bind off.

• *To make up:* Join side seams and shoulder seams. Join sleeve seams and insert sleeves. Using the crochet hook and silk pick up the stitches (see p. 42) around front edges and neck, beginning at the bottom right-hand edge. Work 3 rows in garter stitch. On the first row of this border work 4 baby clothes buttonholes (see p. 45), at regular intervals, on the right front of the cardigan if it is for a boy, on the left front if it is for a girl.

Sew on buttons. Using lurex thread and Swiss darning technique embroider fronts and sleeves as indicated in diagram.

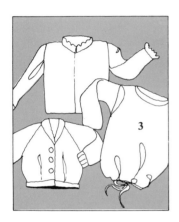

The garments illustrated in colour on p. 128.

Pink lacy top (3)
Illustrated in colour on p. 128

Standard: ★★
Tension: 24 stitches and 25 rows to 10cm(4")

Size: To fit children 2-3 years old. The figures in brackets refer to sizes for 4-5 and 6-7 years.
Materials: 130g(150g–170g)/4oz(5oz–6oz) pink mohair
1 pair needles size 4mm(#6)
1 crochet hook size 3.5mm(#E)
Stitches used: Openwork stitch (see p. 77). Garter stitch (see p. 57). Crocheted bobble border (see p. 44).

Method
• *Back:* Cast on 68(76–84) stitches and work 32(36–40)cm/12½(14–15¾)" in openwork stitch. Work 2 rows in garter stitch. Bind off.
• *Front:* Cast on 72(80–88) stitches and work 28(32–36)cm/11(12½–14)" in openwork stitch. To shape neck bind off the 20(22–24) central stitches; finish both sides separately. On neck edge bind off 2 stitches, then 1 stitch. Bind off remaining stitches.
• *To make up:* Join side seams, leaving opening for sleeves. Stitch shoulder seams. Join sleeve seams and insert sleeves.

Work a crocheted bobble stitch border around neck edge, sleeves and lower edge. Make a single cord (see p. 138) and thread it through the first row of eyelets.

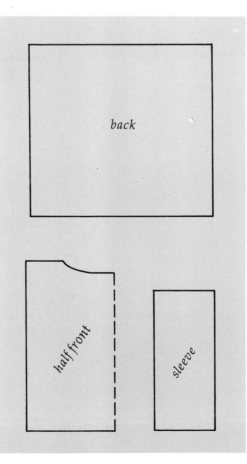

back

half front

sleeve

Special techniques
and finishing touches

Socks and gloves

Socks. Socks are somewhat complicated to make, but with a little patience and practice you will soon achieve satisfactory results.

The great advantage of handknitted socks is that the parts most subject to wear, the heel and the toe, can be re-knitted. Socks are knitted from the top to the toe on four needles, in four stages: the leg (including the border), which can be long or short, the heel, the foot and the toe.

Knitting the leg. The leg is worked as follows: cast on the required number of stitches on a set of four needles and work the border (usually in k.1 p.1 rib, see p. 57) to the depth desired. Continue knitting rounds until the ankle is reached. When knitting knee-socks, shaping for the calf can be done as follows: mark two stitches with a contrast thread and on either side of these decrease one stitch every six rows until the right width is achieved.

Turning the heel. The heel can be turned in various ways: the most common are described here. To reinforce the heel it is a good idea to knit a strong sewing thread of the same colour in with the sock yarn. Remember that even if the leg is knitted in a lacy stitch, the heel should be smooth (i.e. knitted in stockinette stitch or reverse stockinette stitch).

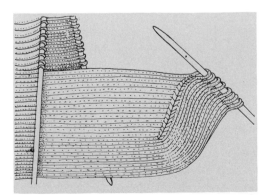

Method 1:
1. Divide the stitches in half; one half will form the heel and the other the front of the sock.
2. Continue working on the heel stitches, on two needles, for 4-6cm (1½-2½″) depending on the size of sock you are knitting.

3. Divide these stitches into three equal parts; leave the two side groups of stitches and continue knitting on the central group only, taking one stitch from each of the side groups on each row (knit the last stitch of the side group together with the first of the central group; pass the last stitch of the central group over the first of the side group) until all the side stitches have been incorporated.

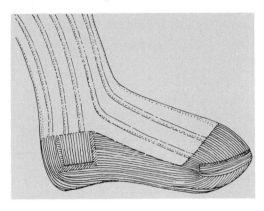

Method 2:
Follow steps 1 and 2 of Method 1.
3. Divide the stitches into three equal groups. Leave the side groups and work twenty rows on the central group in stockinette stitch, knitting the first two stitches and the last two on every row.
4. Pick up and knit the side stitches on the twenty rows worked and continue, taking in one stitch from each of the side groups on each row (as described in step 3 of Method 1) until all the side stitches are incorporated.

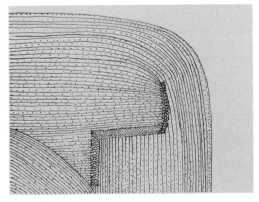

Method 3:
Follow steps 1 and 2 of Method 1.
3. Continue working on the four or five

Socks and gloves can be handknitted very successfully. These and other handknitted garments add a personal touch to your wardrobe. Right: the first stage of turning the heel of a sock (Method 1). Far right, above: a completed heel worked by Method 1. Below: a completed heel worked by Method 2.

central stitches only, leaving the side stitches and taking in one stitch from each side group on every knit row (as described in step 3 of Method 1) until all the side stitches have been incorporated.

Knitting the foot. When the heel has

Right: a completed heel worked by Method 3. Below: a diagram showing the stages in working a sock. Far right, above: the toe worked by Method 1. Below: side view of the toe worked by Method 2.

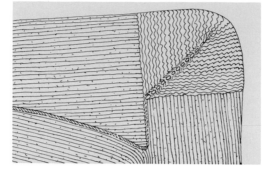

been turned by one of the three methods described above, start knitting the foot. Pick up the side stitches of the heel shaping and start working on four needles again, decreasing one stitch every two or three rows at each side of the upper part of the foot, until the required width is reached, then continue without shaping for the length of the foot minus the toe.

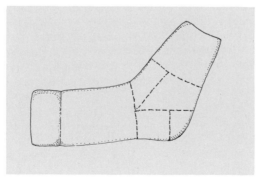

Working the toe. When the foot has been worked, start shaping the toe. Various methods may be used: the most usual are described here. The toe, like the heel, can be reinforced by knitting in a strong thread of the same colour.

Method 1:
1. Divide the stitches into ten equal groups, marking each group with a contrast thread.
2. In the following row decrease one

stitch at each contrast thread.
3. After four or five rows decrease again at the same point.
4. Repeat the decrease row every three

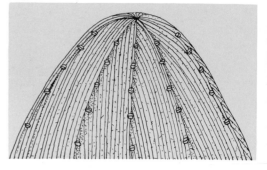

rows until eight stitches remain; bind off these eight stitches thus: knit two together twice, *pass the first stitch over the second, knit two together*; repeat from * to * until all stitches have been bound off. Finish off on the wrong side.

Method 2:
1. Mark the two central stitches of the sole of the foot.
2. Decrease one stitch on either side of the marked stitches on every row, knitting the two stitches preceding the marked stitches together, and working a slip 1, k.1, pass slip stitch over decrease on the two following stitches (see p. 38) until thirty-five or thirty stitches remain.
3. Now start decreasing the upper part of the foot, marking the two central stitches

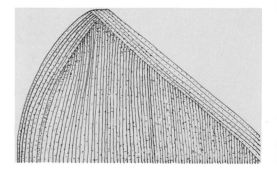

and proceeding as described for the sole.
4. When eight to ten stitches remain, bind off by knitting two together (see step 4, Method 1). Finish off on the wrong side.

Gloves. Gloves with five fingers are knitted on a set of double pointed needles,

Working gloves.
1. Increasing on either side of the two stitches dividing the palm and the back of the glove.
2. Thumb stitches left on a safety pin.
3. Dividing the stitches between four needles to begin knitting a finger.
4 and 5. Closing a finger.

beginning at the wrist. Mittens can be knitted on four or two needles.

Glove pattern. When you have knitted the wrist border, which will generally be in rib, proceed as follows:

1. Continue knitting the main part of the hand for about 2cm(1").

2. Divide the stitches into two equal groups and mark the division with a contrast thread. One group will form the palm of the hand, the other the back.

3. Increase one stitch on either side of the first two stitches of the palm. Continue to increase in the same place every three

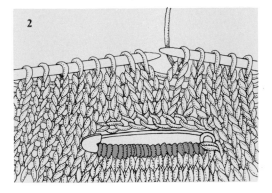

rows until the full breadth of the palm of the hand is reached plus the breadth of the base of the thumb.

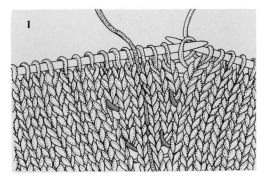

4. Transfer the thumb stitches to a stitch holder, and cast on the same number of stitches.

5. Working across the cast on stitches, continue in rounds until the base of the fingers is reached. Divide the stitches of the back of the hand into four equal groups and divide the stitches of the palm into four corresponding groups. Leaving the stitches for the first finger on the set of four needles, transfer the other groups of

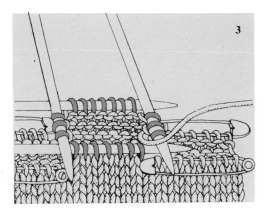

stitches, corresponding to the other fingers, on to separate stitch holders or safety pins.

For the *first finger*, cast on three stitches to join those from the palm and the

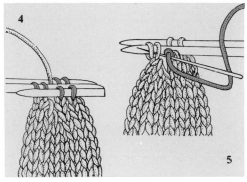

back and work in rounds until the required length is reached. Now knit pairs of stitches together on alternate rounds until two or three stitches are left. Thread the yarn through these stitches, draw up and fasten off on the wrong side.

For the *middle finger*, knit the stitches from the back, pick up and knit three stitches at the base of the first finger, knit the palm stitches and cast on three new stitches. Work in rounds on four needles for the required length and finish off as described for the first finger.

For the *fourth finger*, knit the stitches from the back, pick up and knit three stitches from the base of the middle finger, knit the palm stitches and cast on two new stitches. Work in rounds for the required length, and finish off as described for the first finger.

For the *little finger*, knit the stitches from the back, pick up and knit two stitches from the base of the fourth finger and knit the palm stitches. Work in rounds for the required length and finish off as described for the first finger.

To make the *thumb*, transfer the stitches left on the stitch holder to a needle, pick up the corresponding cast on stitches, and with a set of four needles, work for the required length. Decrease over the

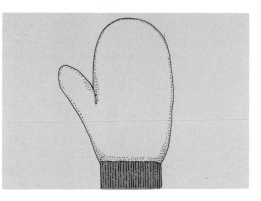

last few rounds until four or five stitches remain; draw the yarn through these and finish off on the wrong side.

Knitting mittens on four needles.

These are worked in the same way as gloves

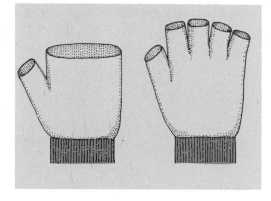

with fingers, but only the thumb is knitted separately. The rest of the mitten is knitted in one piece on four needles to the desired length; the top is shaped by decreasing gradually at each side of the hand until eight stitches remain; draw the yarn through these and finish off on the wrong side.

Knitting fingerless gloves and mittens.

A useful variation on the ordinary versions described above. For the gloves, follow steps 1-5 but when the fingers and thumb are half the normal length, bind off all the

stitches on the needles. The mittens are knitted in a similar manner.

Knitting mittens on two needles.

Cast on the stitches for the wrist border and work the border (generally in rib). Proceed as follows:

1. Work without shaping for a few centimeters (about 1″) until the base of the

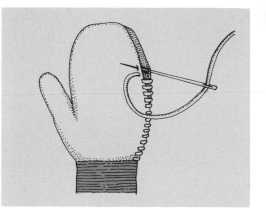

thumb is reached. Working on the two central stitches only, increase one stitch on every knit row on each side of these two stitches until the right number of stitches for the width of the thumb have been made.

2. Continue the thumb without shaping until the desired length is reached.

3. Knit two stitches together on every row until two or three are left. Bind off.

4. Cast on half the number of thumb stitches and continue the main part of the mitten until the required length is reached.

5. Decrease for the top by knitting two stitches together across every row. A more gradual shaping is achieved by knitting two stitches together at the beginning, center and end of each row until four or five stitches remain. Bind off.

6. Sew up the side of the mitten and the thumb on the wrong side of the work.

Finishing touches

Finishing touches such as tassles, pompons, fringes, braids, or embroidery can be used to decorate hand-knitted garments, livening them up with a touch of originality that can lift them out of the ordinary. This is particularly true of embroidery which may be used to striking effect either through cheerful, colourful designs or delicate, soft motifs. Even the addition of a tassle or bobble, or an elegant fringe or braid can transform an ordinary piece of work into a fashion garment, especially when you use your taste and imagination to create something unusual.

How to make tassles. Tassles are often used on scarves, berets etc. To make a tassle you need a rectangular piece of card the same length as your desired tassle. Wrap the yarn around the card until enough has been used for the required thickness of the tassle – each time you wrap the yarn around, this represents two strands of the finished tassle.

Finish the tassle by passing the end of the thread through one end of the tassle and securing it; remove the card and, holding the tassle steady, bind the yarn around the tassle just below the point where you have secured it at the top. Fasten off. Cut the other end evenly, with sharp scissors.

How to make bobbles. Another popular decorative touch, particularly for berets and children's clothes, is a bobble or pompon: a soft ball of threads.

To make a bobble you need two identical discs made of card; their diameter should be about 2cm(1″) more than the desired diameter of the bobble. In the center of the discs cut a hole equivalent to about a quarter of the diameter. For example, if you want to make a 10cm(4″) bobble, your discs should have a diameter of 12cm(5″) and a hole in the middle measuring 3cm(1½″) in diameter. Thread a wool needle with the yarn you are using; holding the discs together carefully, cover with yarn, threading the yarn through the central hole until it is completely filled. Remember that a really compact, dense bobble requires a lot of yarn. When the discs are well covered take a pair of sharp scissors and, pushing the point between

the two discs, cut right round the circumference of the bobble, taking care that the strands of yarn do not pull out of the central hole.

Pull the cardboard discs apart slightly, then wind a double thread around between them and knot it tightly. Leave the ends of the thread so that they may be used to sew the bobble on to the garment. Now remove the cardboard discs, cutting them to make this easier.

Shake the bobble, holding it by the long

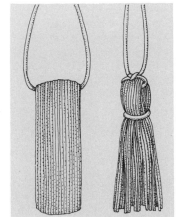

There are a number of finishing touches one can add to a knitted garment, such as tassles and pompons or embroidery. These are useful and imaginative ways of using up odds and ends of yarn.
Above: how to make tassles. Right, three stages in the making of a pompon.

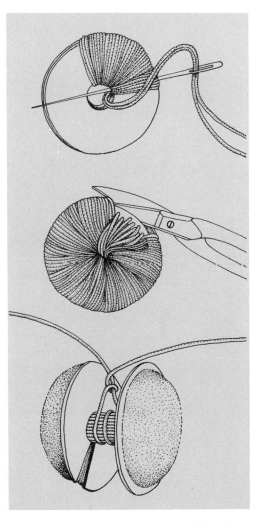

ends of thread, and trim it with sharp scissors.

How to make fringes. Fringes are often used to finish off scarves, shawls and bed covers. They may be made in a variety of ways, of which the following are the most usual.

Simple fringes. Cut the yarn in lengths equal to double the required length of the fringe. Divide these strands into bunches (the number of strands per bunch will depend on the thickness of the yarn and the thickness of the fringe required) and fold in half. Insert a crochet hook through the loop formed by the fold, then through the knitting where the fringe is to be; pull the loop through, then hook the rest of the fringe through the loop with the crochet hook, pulling gently to tighten the knot. Insert each bunch of threads at regular intervals in the same way, threading them through with the crochet hook and pulling them tight. Lastly trim the fringe with a pair of sharp scissors.

Knotted fringes. These are made in the same way as simple fringes, but the strands of yarn should be longer. Then proceed as follows: divide each bunch of threads in half and knot one half to the right-hand half of the neighbouring bunch, working across the whole fringe, taking care that all the knots are at the same height. Second and third knots can be added, alternating the knots and spaces.

How to make cords. Plaited cords are mainly used to tie baby garments such as bibs, bootees, gloves, bonnets etc. They are usually made with the same yarn as was used for the garment, but if the yarn is too thick or unsuitable they can be made from a contrasting yarn.

Twisted cord. To make twisted cord you need a length of yarn about four times the length of the cord you wish to make. Fold the yarn in half and attach the fold to a soft surface such as a cushion, ironing board etc. Then, holding the threads between finger and thumb, begin twisting them from the other end. When they are tightly twisted fold the cord in half again; hold the two ends together and if the operation has been done correctly, the two parts will twist together of their own accord. Make a small knot at either end.

Single plaited cord. You will need three strands of yarn double the length of the cord you wish to make. Knot the three strands together at one end and pin the knot to a soft surface such as a cushion or

ironing board. Plait the strands in the normal way, keeping an even tension.

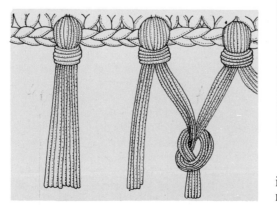

Right, above: making a simple fringe. Right, and far right, above: two stages in the making of a knotted fringe. Far right, below: making a twisted cord.

Double plaited cord. You will need four strands of yarn double the length of the cord you wish to make. Knot the four strands together at one end and pin them

to a soft surface such as a cushion or ironing board. Begin plaiting the strands as follows: working from right to left, pass the first strand over the second, the third under the fourth and over the first. Repeat, always beginning from the right, until all the thread has been plaited.

Looped cord. You will need a strand of yarn eight times as long as the cord you intend to make; fold the yarn in half. At

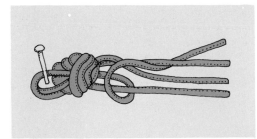

the fold make a loop with the index finger of the left hand and a loop with the index finger of the right hand, then thread the right-hand loop through the left-hand one from front to back; take up the resulting loop with the index finger of the right hand and pull the left-hand thread

to tighten it. Make another loop on the left-hand thread with the index finger of the left hand and thread it through the right-hand loop from front to back; take up the resulting loop with the left hand and pull the right-hand thread to tighten it. Continue in this way, making a new loop on the strand that has just been tightened.

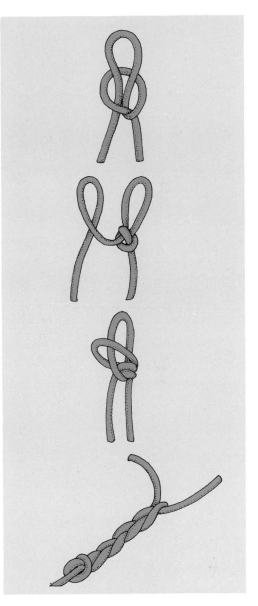

Embroidery on knitting. Knitted garments can easily be embroidered with very effective results.

Swiss darning. The stitches described below are intended specifically for embroidery on knitting. A stockinette stitch background is best suited to this type of embroidery. Each stitch is covered by an embroidered stitch which follows the same shape.

Swiss darning may be used as a substitute for Jacquard knitting, thus avoiding the need to use several colours at once while the knitting is in progress.

When working Swiss darning you should use yarn of the same thickness as the background in order to cover the background stitches perfectly.

This type of embroidery doubles the thickness of the original knitting and it is therefore an excellent method of disguising threadbare, stained or faded patches.

A motif in Swiss darning is worked by following a design drawn on graph paper such as those used for Jacquard knitting (see p. 52, or you can make your own designs). Each square of the chart corresponds to one stitch of the knitting and to one complete embroidery stitch. It is important not to pull the threads too tight or you will pucker the knitted background. Swiss darning may be worked horizontally or vertically.

Horizontal Swiss darning. Horizontal Swiss darning is worked as follows:
1. Fasten the thread on the wrong side of the work and pass the needle through to the right side at the base of the first stitch to be embroidered.
2. Pass the needle from right to left behind the vertical threads of the stitch in the row above that to be embroidered, bringing it out at the top left-hand corner of the first stitch. The right-hand thread will now be covered.

3. Pass the needle through the base of the first stitch and bring it out at the base of the next stitch, thus covering the left-hand thread of the first stitch.

Repeat steps 2 and 3 across the first row. Turn the work to embroider the second row (and subsequent even rows) in the same way.

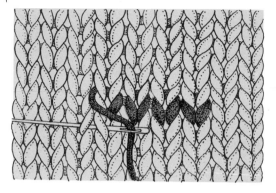

Vertical Swiss darning. Vertical Swiss darning is worked as follows:
1. Fasten the thread on the wrong side of the work and pass the needle through the center of the stitch below that to be covered.
2. Pass the needle behind the vertical

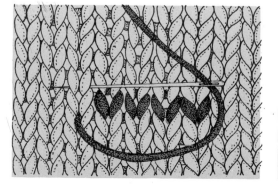

Right, and far right, above: two stages in horizontal Swiss darning on stockinette stitch. Far right, below: two stages in vertical Swiss darning.

threads of the stitch in the row above the relevant stitch, thus covering the right-hand thread.

3. Insert the needle at the point where you began and bring it out above the horizontal thread, in the center of the stitch which is now completely covered.

Repeat steps 2 and 3 until the required number of stitches have been embroidered.

Knot stitch motifs. Knot stitch motifs are highly decorative and can be worked with contrasting yarns which stand out against knitted backgrounds. A pattern of small flowers, worked as follows, is one of the most popular designs: bring the needle from the wrong side to the right side of the work where the center of the flower will be; pull the thread through. Put the needle back through the knitting very close to the center and bring it out where the tip of the first petal will be. Wind the thread several times around the needle, then insert the needle at the central point again, bringing it out where the tip of the second petal will be; wind the thread around again, pass the needle through the center and so on, until all the petals have been worked.

Finish off the thread on the wrong side of the work, at the center of the flower, with several small stitches.

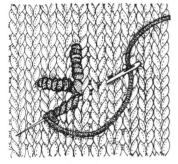

Above: embroidering a flower in knot stitch. Right, and far right, top: three stages in smocking. Far right, below: finished smocking.

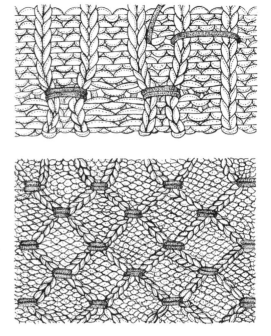

Smocking. Smocking can be worked over the following ribbed pattern:

Row 1 and odd rows (right side of work): *p.3, k.1*, p.3.

Row 2 and even rows (wrong side of work): *k.3, p.1*, k.3.

When you have worked the required length of knitting in the above stitch, work the smocking horizontally; it is usually worked in a contrasting colour, as follows:

Line 1: fasten the thread on the wrong side of the work and bring the needle through to the right side on the fifth row, immediately before the second knit rib. Pass the needle through the work again immediately after the third knit rib and bring it out where you began. Insert it at the same point after the third rib and bring it out before the fourth. Tighten the stitches thus made to pull the second and third lines of knit stitches together. Continue across the work drawing the vertical lines together in pairs. Fasten off the thread on the wrong side of the work.

Line 2: begin on the right-hand side again, five rows above the first line of smocking and alternate the smocking as follows: pull together the first and second knit ribs, the third and fourth and so on across the work.

Repeat as often as required, alternating lines 1 and 2.

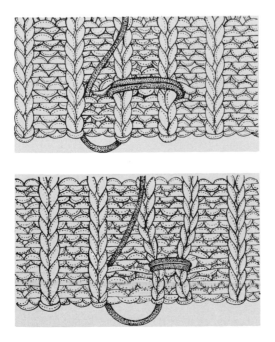

141

Making up

Pressing and sewing up are the last things that have to be done when the various pieces of a garment have been knitted. For a successful result these two final operations must be done with great care. The illustrations show how the pieces of a knitted garment should be blocked and pressed.

Making up includes all the finishing that has to be done when a piece of knitting is completed: putting in the zipper, sewing seams, pressing etc. This does not deal with embellishments or decoration, but with essential structural work on which the success of the final result depends. Making up deserves great care and attention: it may be possible to cover up some small defects in the knitting when finishing the garment, notably when sewing the seams, but if the making up is badly or carelessly done, it can ruin the final garment to a greater extent than a mistake in the knitting.

Pressing the pieces. Once all the different pieces of a garment have been knitted they should be pressed. This is a very important stage of the work and the yarn and stitches used should be taken into account. Some yarns, like cotton and linen, should be pressed with a hot iron. Others, like wool, should be steamed; synthetics require a cool iron or should not be pressed at all. Instructions for the pressing of a particular yarn are generally given on the ball-band and should be followed scrupulously.

As regards different stitches some, like cable, rib, garter stitch and most relief stitches, should not be pressed. Others, like stockinette stitch, require pressing, provided the type of yarn permits it.

When pieces of knitting are being ironed, care must be taken not to press them out of shape or to alter their measurements. The following advice will help you to avoid mishaps: lay the piece to be pressed on a flat surface large enough to accommodate it, right side down. Pin the piece to the correct shape, checking the measurements with a tape measure against those of the pattern.

If the yarn requires it, place a damp cloth over the knitting before pressing it and set the iron at the right temperature (see the ball-band for information). The iron should not be pushed to and fro in the normal way; it should be placed in one spot, pressed down for a few seconds and then lifted and placed in another spot and so on until the whole piece has been pressed. If a damp cloth has been used, it should be completely dry by the time the pressing is completed.

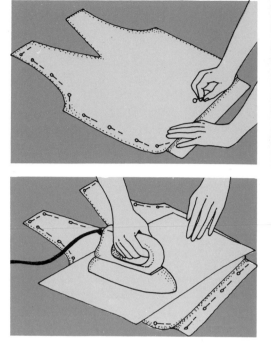

Knitting made from yarns that should not be pressed can be blocked out and pinned, covered with a slightly damp cloth and left until the cloth is completely dry.

Careful pressing can correct small errors of shaping and straighten up darts, armholes, increasing and decreasing etc.

Sewing up. When the pieces have been pressed, they are sewn together and the success of the finished garment depends to a large extent on how this is done.

There are various kinds of seam: choose the one most suited to the stitch used, the garment you are making and your degree of experience, and stitch the seams as carefully as possible, without distorting the shape.

Backstitch. The most common stitch used for shoulders, side seams and sleeves. It is not suitable for very bulky yarns nor for highly textured stitches. It is done with a blunt wool needle which will not split the wool; if such a needle is not available use a normal needle, sewing with the eye rather than with the point.

Backstitch is worked as follows: place the two pieces to be sewn right sides together, making sure that the ends meet perfectly; pin both ends together. Start sewing from the right, inserting the needle from front to back and then from back to front in the next stitch to the left. Pass the needle from front to back again, at the point where you began and bring it out two stitches to the left. Subsequent stitches are made from front to back at the end of the preceding stitch and from back to front through the next stitch to the left. Fasten off the thread. While sewing the thread should not be pulled so that the stitches are tight, as this can pull the knitting out of shape.

On the wrong side this seam makes a

Right: sewing a seam with back stitch. Right below: overcasting a seam. Far right, above: a vertical invisible seam. Below: grafting.

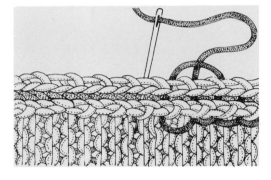

straight line; if done well it is very strong and is invisible on the right side of the work.

Backstitch can also be used to reduce the size of the pieces of a garment at the seams, if they are too big. In this case the seam should not be more than 1cm(½″) away from the edge.

Overcasting. This is especially suitable for borders, relief stitches, and thick, bulky yarns.

Place the two pieces to be sewn right sides together with ends matching; pin both ends together. Work in a close

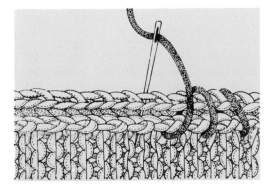

overcast stitch without pulling the stitches too tight, as follows: insert the needle at the back of the work and bring it through to the front. Work from right to left and make sure the two pieces match exactly.

This seam is strong and will not lose its shape; on the right side it creates a corded effect.

Vertical invisible seam. Usually used for side seams and for putting in sleeves. It is virtually invisible on stockinette stitch. It is worked in the following way: place the edges side by side, right sides up, pinning the upper edges together. Fasten the edges at the bottom with a small stitch. The seam is worked from bottom to top. Insert the needle in the center of the first stitch on the right-hand piece from the right side; bring the needle out through the center of the first stitch on the left-hand piece. Pass the needle under the horizontal stitch just formed. Continue to

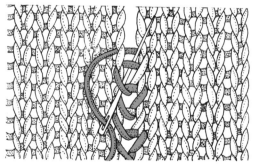

pass the needle from right to left then under the horizontal stitch to the end of the seam.

Grafting. Used to join two pieces of knitting in stockinette stitch horizontally. It is worked on the right side of the

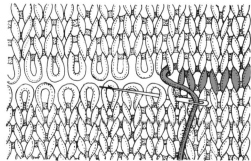

knitting on an edge that has not been bound off; the stitches should be ironed lightly to prevent them from unravelling.

Place the two edges together, matching the ends and pinning the left-hand end. Secure the thread at the right and start the seam by inserting the needle through the first stitch of the upper piece. Bring the thread through the second stitch, insert the needle into the first stitch of the lower piece and bring it out through the second stitch. Insert the needle into the stitch last worked of the upper piece (the second stitch) and bring it out through the third. Repeat on the lower edge and proceed in this way until the seam is completed.

A similar seam can be worked with the stitches on the needles; hold the two needles together, insert the needle into the stitches as described above and slip them off the needle.

Putting in a zipper. One of the most convenient methods of fastening garments, even if they are knitted, is a zipper. This is frequently used instead of loops or buttons, particularly on skirts, but also on jumpers, cardigans and jackets. Zippers which are closed at one end are used for skirts, the neck openings of jumpers etc.; open-ended zippers which have a clasp at the bottom are used for jackets and cardigans.

A normal dressmaker's zipper is suitable for most types of knitted garment. The heavier, stronger zippers (usually the ones that open at the bottom) are used for heavy knitwear and sportswear. Carefully measure the length of the opening and when you have decided on the type of zipper to use and found the colour to match the garment, ensure that the zipper is the same length as the opening (only the metal part of the zipper counts, not the extra tape at the bottom). If the zipper is too short the seam will pucker, if it is too long the edges of the opening will stretch.

A zipper is inserted as follows: fit the zipper into the opening on the wrong side of the work and pin it into place on the right side. The teeth of the zipper should be just level with the edges of the opening; when the zipper is closed the edges should meet exactly. Tack on the right side of the work and remove the pins;

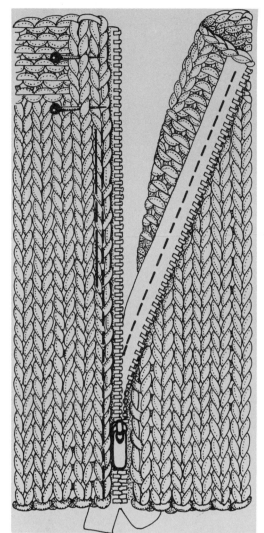

open the zipper and stitch it in using an embroidery needle and thread the same colour as the tape. With the thread on the wrong side of the work at the top right-hand corner stitch as close to the knitted edge as possible in the following way: pull the thread through the work, then pull it through to the back again slightly to the right, then forward again about 5mm (a fraction of an inch) to the left of the preceding stitch, then through to the back and so on.

The stitches will be invisible on the right side of the work because the fine thread disappears into the knitting. On the wrong side long stitches similar to machine stitching will be visible on the tape. When one side has been stitched, if the zipper is closed at the bottom, fasten the tape at the base with a couple of stitches, then sew up the other side in the same way as the first.

To finish off on the wrong side, fold the tops of the tape back and stitch them to the edge of the work so that they do not get in the way of the zipper. Using the appropriate coloured thread overcast (see p. 143) around the edge including the folded ends. The zipper must open and close with ease. If the zipper catches it may be because the stitches have been worked too near the teeth.

Opposite: how to sew in a zipper. Right: sewing on grosgrain ribbon. Far right, above: applying a leather or suede patch. Below: applying a fabric patch.

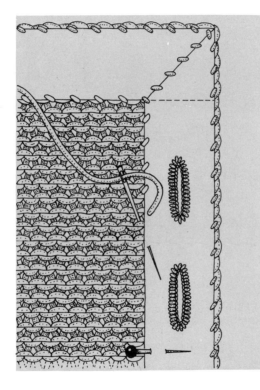

How to sew on reinforcing tape. To strengthen the edges of cardigans and jackets, particularly where there are buttons and buttonholes, a grosgrain ribbon can be stitched on the inside.

Turn the ends of the grosgrain in and pin the ribbon along the length of the inside edge, taking care that no ribbon can be seen from the outside, and ensuring that you do not distort the tension of the knitting.

Stitch the ribbon in place with the appropriate coloured thread using the same stitch as that described for inserting zippers (see p. 144). Having stitched all around the outside edge, mark the buttonholes with pins corresponding to the holes in the knitting; if no buttonholes have yet been made, position them at regular intervals. Make a slit in the ribbon and stitch around with buttonhole stitch as follows: pass the needle from front to back just below the edge of the buttonhole, coming out on the wrong side; pass the needle through from front to back once again, passing the thread under the tip of the needle from left to right, and tighten the thread gently, so that the stitches lie flat.

If the grosgrain has to go around a corner, first sew the outer edge, then fold the ribbon at an angle and fasten it before stitching the inside edge.

Patching. A popular way of reinforcing the areas that get the most wear (elbows, knees etc.) or of hiding a hole is to sew on patches. Leather or suede patches can be purchased; decorative fabric patches can be made at home, to match the garment or to contrast with it. Bought patches come in various sizes, for children or adults, and they generally have little holes punched around the edge to make sewing them on easier.

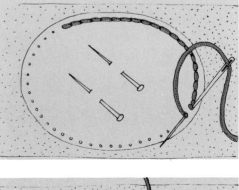

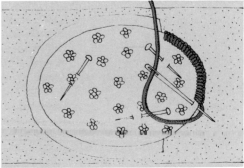

A patch is applied as follows: pin it on to the garment, putting pins through the center as well as around the edge; take care neither to stretch it, nor to put it on too loosely. With a needle and thread of the right colour begin sewing on the right side with the same stitch as used for sewing in zippers (see p. 144), stitching through every hole to form a continuous line of stitching round the patch. If the patch is made of fabric use the following method: fold in a border of ½cm(¼") on the inside and tack. Pin the patch in place and stitch it on with buttonhole stitch (see above). If patching elbows, the second patch should be sewn on in the same way as the first, care being taken to make it perfectly symmetrical.

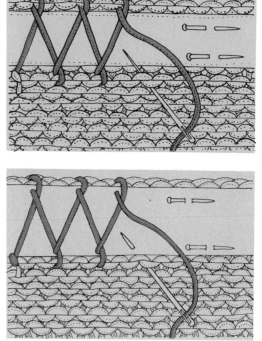

Right: making a loop such as would be used for a belt. Far right: a waistband finished with elastic and herringbone stitch; above, the stitching allows the elastic to move freely; below, by catching the edge of the elastic it is fastened to the garment.

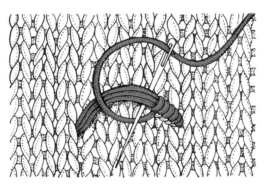

Making loops for belts. When a knitted garment has a separate belt it is a good idea to make loops on the side seams of the garment.

Loops for belts can be knitted, using the same stitch as for the garment, and then sewn on, or they can be sewn with matching thread directly on to the garment. Stitched loops are made in the following way: secure the thread at the back of the knitting where the belt is to be and bring the needle through to the front. Make four or five loose vertical stitches, slightly longer than the width of the belt. Beginning at one end cover these stitches closely with buttonhole stitch (see p. 145).

Inserting elastic with herringbone stitch. A convenient way of finishing the waist of a skirt is to stitch elastic on the inside. The elastic should be at least 2cm(1") wide. It is inserted as follows:

establish the desired waist measurement of the skirt and cut the elastic to that length allowing 2cm(1") extra for the seam. Overlap the two ends and overcast them (see p. 143).

Divide the elastic into five equal parts, marking each one with a pin. Turn the skirt inside out and divide the waist into five equal parts. Matching pins, tack the elastic into place and remove the pins.

Work around the waist in herringbone stitch as follows: using a wool needle and the yarn used for the skirt secure the yarn above the elastic at a side seam. Working from left to right, bring the thread diagonally down across the elastic and take a horizontal stitch from right to left below the lower edge of the elastic through two stitches of the garment but not through the elastic. Continue in the same way moving diagonally from top to bottom and bottom to top right around the waist; the elastic is thus able to move freely inside the herringbone stitch. Alternatively it can be fastened to the skirt by taking in a bit of the edge of the elastic on each horizontal stitch.

Correcting mistakes and renovating

In knitting, as in all handwork, practice and experience will help you to overcome the diffidence you may feel when confronted with yarn and knitting needles for the first time. You will realize that making mistakes is not a disaster; most mistakes are easy to rectify if you know the basic techniques. You will also come to realize that when the finished article no longer pleases, it can be undone and the yarn re-used, or it can be lengthened, shortened or modified in a variety of ways. If it gets torn or develops holes there is no need to throw it away: it can be mended. Some of these tricks of the trade are described in the following pages, others you will invent for yourself.

Picking up a dropped knit stitch. If you notice that a knit stitch has been dropped on the previous row you can pick it up again as follows: the dropped stitch and the horizontal thread should be picked up from the front and placed on the right-hand needle. Insert the left-hand needle into the stitch from behind. With the right-hand needle pass the horizontal thread through the stitch, thus re-forming the dropped stitch. The stitch will be on the right-hand needle, the wrong way round; transfer it to the left hand needle and continue knitting.

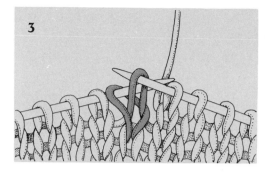

Picking up a dropped purl stitch. If you notice that a purl stitch has been dropped in the previous row you can pick it up again as follows: the dropped stitch and the horizontal thread should be picked up from the back and placed on the right-hand needle. Insert the left-hand needle into the stitch from the front. With the right-hand needle pass the horizontal thread through the stitch, and slip the

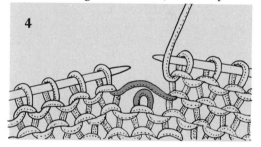

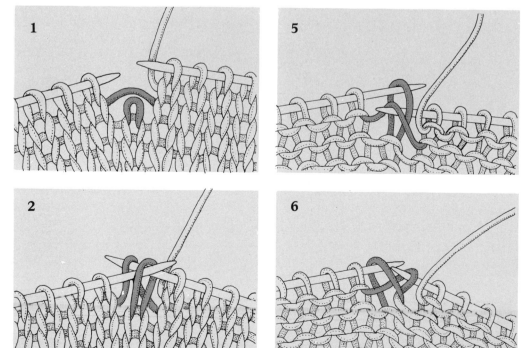

Correcting mistakes, altering, lengthening or shortening a garment are all important tricks of the trade. Making a mistake need not be a disaster since most mistakes can be corrected quite easily. 1, 2 and 3. Picking up a stitch on the right side of the work. 4, 5 and 6. Picking up a stitch on the wrong side of the work.

stitch off the left-hand needle. The new stitch will be on the right-hand needle and should be transferred to the left-hand needle; continue knitting as usual.

How to pick up a dropped stitch several rows down. When a dropped stitch is not picked up for several rows the unworked

1. and 2. Picking up a stitch from several rows down on the right side of the work. 3. and 4. Picking up a stitch from several rows down on the wrong side of the work. 5. Undoing a stitch.

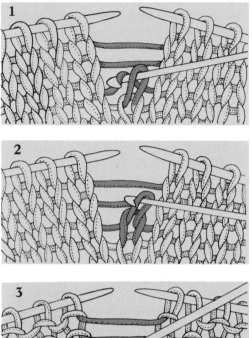

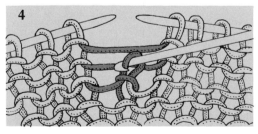

threads above the dropped stitch form a kind of ladder. This often happens when the knitting is put down in the middle of a row; if the stitch being knitted is very complicated, with eyelets and increasing etc. it is very difficult to remedy. But if you are knitting in a stitch consisting of knit and purl the mistake can be rectified.

To pick up *knit stitches* on the right side, insert a crochet hook into the

dropped stitch from the front, then catch the horizontal thread in the row above and pull it through the stitch, forming a new stitch. Repeat until all the stitches on all the rows have been re-formed: the ladder will have disappeared. If there are other dropped stitches in the work it is a good idea to secure them with a safety pin while you are coping with the first one; this prevents them from unravelling further.

Picking up *purl stitches* is a little more difficult because, having inserted the crochet hook into the loop of the dropped stitch from the back and passed the horizontal thread through it to form the new stitch (as illustrated) you have to remove the hook and insert it again from the back to catch the thread of the row above.

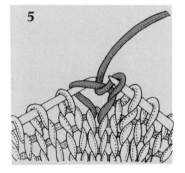

How to unpick rows. If you notice a mistake in a previous row you can unpick stitches by inserting the left-hand needle into the stitch of the previous row (see illustration), continuing until the error is reached.

Knitting too many rows. It may happen that you lose count of the rows and knit a few rows too many. This can be rectified as follows: pick up the thread of a stitch in the middle of the piece of knitting and pull it sharply, then cut the thread at the left-hand side of the work. The knitting will come apart. Undo the last stitches on the left-hand side, then cut the thread on the right-hand side, and undo the last few stitches to free the thread. If you want to rejoin the two pieces put the stitches of the upper part on to a needle, undo the required number of rows on the lower part and put these stitches on to a needle as well. Now hold the two needles

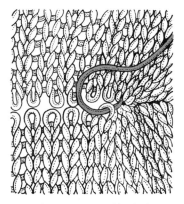

Dividing a piece of knitting where too many rows have been worked.

together and join the stitches by grafting (see p. 143). The join will be invisible.

This system can be used for lengthening as well as shortening jumpers, for renewing ribbed waistbands and wristbands and renovating knitwear. When the knitting has been opened and the upper stitches picked up a new ribbed edge can be knitted, or the required number of rows can be worked on the lower stitches.

Mending knitwear. A knitted garment which has been worn for a long period can wear thin in places (the elbows of a jumper for example); or it may develop holes which require mending. Worn-out patches and holes are darned.

Darning is done in two stages: first the threads are laid across the hole or worn patch, and they are then darned. There are two methods of darning, which differ in how the threads are laid. The illustrations show the two methods for darning the right side of stockinette stitch.

Darning stockinette stitch on the right side using horizontal threads. This is the first method of darning. On the wrong side of the work make one horizontal thread per row to be darned. Having done

so, thread a wool needle and bring the thread to the front of the work on the left-hand side, through a stitch at the edge of the darn. Next, working from bottom to top and holding the thread to the left of the needle as you work, insert the needle below the bottom horizontal thread, bringing it out above it, then under the next one and so on. When you reach the last horizontal thread pass the needle, working from top to bottom, to the left of the nearest stitch and then pass it to the right of the stitch it has just been through. Work from bottom to top as before, putting the needle under each horizontal thread as illustrated and always holding the thread to the left of the needle. When you reach the stitch you originally started from, draw the thread through the next stitch on the right and start a new row from top to bottom. Continue until the darn is complete.

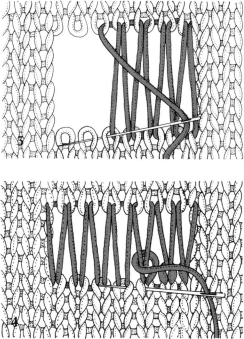

Darning stockinette stitch on the right side using vertical threads. The second method of darning is worked over vertical threads. To prepare the hole, work in and out of the upper and lower stitches as illustrated. The number and length of the threads should equal the number of the missing stitches and rows. When this first stage is complete, thread a wool needle

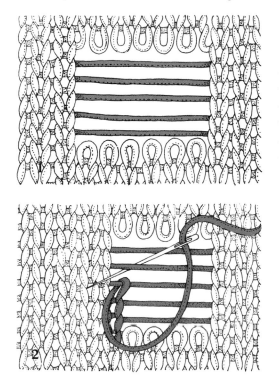

Darning over horizontal threads: 1. Preparation of the hole; 2. Darning back over the threads from bottom to top. 3. and 4. Darning over vertical threads.

with yarn of the same colour as the garment but which is slightly finer and secure it on the wrong side of the work. Bring the needle to the right side through the center of the bottom left-hand stitch and, working from left to right, pass the needle behind the two vertical threads of that stitch, then insert it into the same stitch again, and bring it out through the next stitch along. Continue in this way over the whole of the first row, then work the return row in the same way but from right to left as illustrated. The darned stitches should look as much like the ordinary stitches as possible.

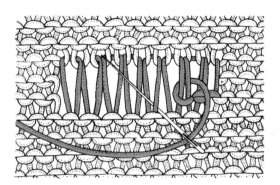

Darning on the wrong side using vertical threads. Prepare the vertical threads for darning on the wrong side as described above. The second stage is worked horizontally, inserting the needle to the right of the two vertical threads which come from each stitch and pulling it through to the left.

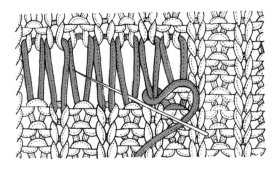

Right, above: darning a purl row over vertical threads. Below: darning single rib. Far right: making a skein over the back of a chair.

Darning single rib. Single rib is darned using the vertical thread method. The preparation of the threads is carried out as described for darning stockinette stitch. Then work one stitch as for stockinette stitch (knit) and one stitch as for purl.

Undoing knitted garments. If a knitted garment is no longer used – because it is out of fashion or it no longer fits – and the yarn is still in good condition, the garment can be unpicked and the yarn

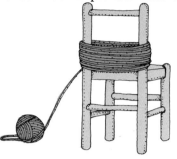

reused. First undo all the seams and divide the garment into separate pieces using sharp, pointed scissors, cutting one or two of the seam stitches at a time. If one or two stitches at the edge of the work should in fact be cut it does not really matter: it will mean when you unpick that part, the yarn will be broken and you will have to start a new ball.

Once all the seams have been undone and you have removed any borders, collars, pockets etc., unravelling can begin. Always start from the end of a piece, where it was bound off, and work towards the beginning. It is a good idea to wind the wool, which is curly from having been knitted, into balls straight away to prevent it getting tangled. When you come to a break in the yarn, as was mentioned above, start a new ball; do not make knots or joins.

If there are worn areas in the garment the yarn from those parts should be wound separately from the rest, since it should not be used for knitting new garments; it can be used for sewing up.

Once the whole garment has been unravelled, the balls should be wound off into skeins; to do this without help attach the end of the yarn to the back of a chair and make a skein round the chair keeping an even tension.

Washing skeins of used wool. Used wool should be immersed in plenty of warm water to which a little soap powder or detergent has been added. Leave the skeins for a few hours, until the crinkled effect has disappeared, then rinse several times. Thread the skeins (without squeez-

ing them) on to a support and leave them to dry away from direct heat. When the yarn is completely dry it can be wound into balls again and reused.

Using odds and ends for striped knitting. Knitting in coloured stripes produces an attractive effect and allows one to use up scraps of wool in a decorative way. The odds and ends must naturally all be of the same thickness. Stripes can be horizontal, vertical, diagonal or zig-zag. They are usually knitted in stockinette stitch but garter stitch and rib can be used effectively as well.

Knitting horizontal stripes. If the horizontal stripes are based on an *even* number of rows knit as normal, changing colours at the right-hand edge of the work and leaving the colour not in use there until it is needed; it should be carried between stripes quite loosely or it will pucker the edge of the work.

If the horizontal stripes are based on an *uneven* number of rows, use double pointed needles. Work as follows for

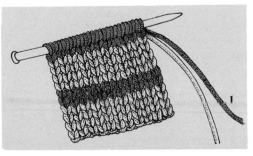

Knitting stripes with odds and ends of wool. 1. Knitting horizontal stripes with an even number of rows. 2. Knitting horizontal stripes with an uneven number of rows. 3. Knitting vertical stripes.

stripes three rows wide:
Rows 1, 2 and 3: work with colour 1.
Rows 4, 5 and 6: work with colour 2.
Row 7: work with colour 1, but do not turn the work: begin knitting from the opposite end of the needle (where colour 1 is waiting).
Rows 8 and 9: work with colour 1.
Row 10: work with colour 2, in the same way as row 7.

The colour change rows are knitted in the same stitch as the preceding row, i.e. on stockinette stitch purl if the previous row was purl, knit if it was knit.

Knitting vertical stripes. To knit vertical stripes the same number of balls of yarn as there are colours must be used per row. The yarn not in use is passed along the

back of the work, either in a loop or woven in depending on the breadth of the blocks of colour, as in Jacquard knitting (see pp. 52-3).

Knitting diagonal stripes. Diagonal stripes are knitted in the same way as vertical stripes but on each row the colours are moved along by one or more stitches to the left or right.

Knitting zig-zag stripes. To achieve a zig-zag effect knit diagonals in one direction then change direction and work the same number of rows.

Some useful tips

We give a few hints and suggestions here which may be useful during the different phases of producing a garment – knitting, making up and the subsequent care of the garment. These are small hints from personal experience; you will be able to add your own ideas.

• It is a good idea to buy one or two extra balls of yarn; they will always come in useful later for darning, renovating, or lengthening.

• It is best to work with thread coming from the center of the ball of yarn. To find the end press your thumb and first finger into the middle of the ball, pull out some yarn, locate the end and, if the yarn is tangled, untangle the yarn and start knitting. This might appear to be a waste of time but in fact it is not, because while you are knitting you do not have to keep stopping to unwind the ball.

• When making an inset pocket on a garment using thick wool it is a good idea to knit only a few centimeters (an inch or so) with the thick yarn and to then continue with finer yarn (changing needles of course); this prevents the thickness of the pocket from spoiling the shape of the garment.

• If the finish on buttonholes is not perfect you can work a border of buttonhole stitch around each one, using matching embroidery thread.

• If you are an experienced knitter it is a good idea to knit baby clothes (particularly the sleeves, which are soon outgrown) from top to bottom, inverting the instructions. As the binding off will thus be at the bottom edge it is very simple to undo the edge and lengthen the garment, using a spare piece of the same wool.

• Another useful tip is to make wide hems on childrens' clothes so that they can be lengthened without difficulty.

• It is not advisable to make knots in the middle of the row as they can spoil the texture of the knitting. Try to start a new ball at the end of a row, remembering that one row requires a length of yarn from two to four times the width of the knitting.

• Knitted garments tend to stretch and lose their shape easily where they are tightest. It is a good rule to line skirts and trousers to knee level.

On jackets and coats the shoulder seam and the back of the collar should always be reinforced with a matching tape. Put a tape for hanging a coat or jacket at the back of the neck, otherwise the shoulders may be pulled out of shape. Remember that garments made in stockinette stitch lose their shape and stretch more than others, so try not to leave them hanging up.

• Whether or not a knitted garment wears well also depends on the way it is washed. Washing instructions are usually given on the ball-band of the yarn.

Conversion tables for European and US sizes

In most countries, there tends to be no exact correspondence between the sizes in general use and the actual measurements of garments produced by different manufacturers. The table of European and American sizes given below gives the equivalent conventional measurements, but it would be wise to remember that the variation between the standard sizes and the actual measurements of a garment may be more marked in one country than another; these differences may be due to commercial requirements, or to changes in fashion.

COUNTRY	MEN'S SIZES						
ITALY	42	44	46	48	50	52	54
GERMANY SWITZERLAND HOLLAND	44	46	48	50	52	54	56
FRANCE BELGIUM	38	40	42	44	46	48	50
GREAT BRITAIN	32	34	36	38	40	42	44
U.S.A. CANADA	34	36	38	40	42	44	46
SPAIN	32	34	36	38	40	42	44

COUNTRY	WOMEN'S SIZES								
ITALY	38	40	42	44	46	48	50	52	54
GERMANY SWITZERLAND HOLLAND	34	36	38	40	42	44	46	48	50
FRANCE BELGIUM	36	38	40	42	44	46	48	50	52
GREAT BRITAIN	32 6	34 8	36 10	38 12	40 14	42 16	44 18	46 20	48 22
U.S.A.	28 2	30 4	32 6	34 8	36 10	38 12	40 14	42 16	44 18
CANADA	28	30	32	34	36	38	40	42	44
SPAIN	30	32	34	36	38	40	42	44	46

Many garments nowadays use one of the American systems of sizing, which substitutes abbreviations for numerical sizing; in fact this system could be considered international. The sizes are as follows: XS/extra small, S/small, M/medium, L/large, XL/extra large, XXL/extra extra large. The following table gives the corresponding Italian sizes.

COUNTRY	WOMEN'S SIZES				
ITALY	38	40-42	44-46	48-50	52-54
U.S.A.	XS	S	M	L	XL

COUNTRY	MEN'S SIZES				
ITALY	42-44	46-48	48-50	52	54
U.S.A.	S	M	L	XL	XXL

Stains and stain removal

STAIN	FABRIC	TREATMENT AND SOLVENTS
Beer	All fabrics	Rinse in water and alcohol.
Blood	All fabrics	Soak in cold water, then wash.
Burns	All fabrics	Lighten the burnt fibers with a 3% solution of hydrogen peroxide.
Chocolate	All fabrics	Dab with glycerine, then wash with water and alcohol.
Coca-Cola	All fabrics	Moisten the stain, then rinse and if necessary treat with ethylene tricholorate.
Cocoa	All fabrics	Dab with glycerine, then wash with water and alcohol.
Coffee	All fabrics	Rub with glycerine, then wash with water containing a little ammonia.
Cosmetics (non oil-based)	All fabrics	Wash immediately with soap and water.
Cosmetics (oil-based)	All fabrics	See Grease.
Cream	All fabrics	Wash with hot water and ammonia. Old stains should be softened in water and borax.
Egg white	All fabrics	If dry, soften in cold water, then wash.
Egg yolk	All fabrics	Wash with soap and water and a little ammonia.
Foundation (tinted)	All fabrics	Wash immediately with lukewarm water. In more serious cases clean with trichloride or tetrachloride.
Fruit, fruit juice	All fabrics	Light stains should be washed immediately with soap and water. Dark stains should be soaked in lemon juice, citric acid or acetic acid.
Glue (cellulose)	All fabrics	Soften with hot water and rub with ether and alcohol.
Glue (gum arabic)	All fabrics	Soften with hot water, then wash with lukewarm water and ammonia.
Glue (wood)	All fabrics	Wash with hot water and soap and rinse with water.
Grass	All fabrics except silk	Rub with a solution of 2 parts alcohol, 1 part ammonia and 3 parts hot water.
Grass	Silk	Soak in a 2% solution of hydrogen peroxide and pour a few drops of ammonia on the stain.
Grease	Cotton	Place the stain over an absorbent surface and dab with one of the following solvents: benzine, trichloride, tetrachloride, or magnesium benzolate.
Grease	Linen	Sprinkle the stain with chalk, magnesium or borax, cover with absorbent paper and iron with a cool iron. The same solvents as indicated for cotton can be used.
Grease	Man-made	Wash with soap and water, or dab with trichloride, benzine or tetrachloride.
Grease	Silk	Sprinkle the stain with chalk, magnesium or borax, cover with absorbent paper and iron with a cool iron. Repeat treatment as often as necessary.

STAIN	FABRIC	TREATMENT AND SOLVENTS
Grease	Wool	Fresh stains can be washed with soap and warm water with a little ammonia. Treat old stains as for cotton.
Ice cream	All fabrics	Fresh stains should be rinsed in water immediately. Old stains should be treated with a solution of water and borax (10 g borax per quart of water) then with trichloride or tetrachloride.
Ink	Cotton and man-made fibers	Dab with a drop of bleach on cotton wool. Wash immediately (dyed cotton may fade).
Ink	Wool and silk	Wash out with water, then rub with lemon juice or citric acid.
Ink (copier)	All fabrics	Place stain over an absorbent surface and treat with trichloride, tetrachloride or alcohol.
Ink (Indian, printer's)	All fabrics	Fresh stains are soluble in water and ammonia. Old stains should be softened in the same solution, then treated with a good stain remover.
Ink (red)	All fabrics	Place stain over an absorbent surface and treat with ether and alcohol in equal proportions.
Jam	All fabrics	First soak in hot water, then treat as for fruit stains.
Milk	All fabrics	Fresh stains should be moistened with benzine, sprinkled with magnesium and left for some hours, then washed in lukewarm water. Old stains should be softened first in water and borax.
Nicotine	All fabrics	Treat with equal parts of glycerine and ammonia; rinse well.
Paint (gloss)	All fabrics	Treat with turpentine.
Pen (ballpoint)	All fabrics	Place stain over an absorbent surface and treat with trichloride, tetrachloride or alcohol.
Perfume	All fabrics	Dab with alcohol then wash in lukewarm water, or treat with trichloride or tetrachloride.
Rubber stamp	All fabrics	Place stain over an absorbent surface and treat with trichloride, tetrachloride or alcohol.
Rust	All fabrics	Soak the stain in a solution of 2 g sorrel salts dissolved in a quart of distilled water to which 10 g glycerine should be added. Leave for several hours, rubbing from time to time, then wash in hot water.
Tar	All fabrics	Soften hard stains with oil, then rub with turpentine to which 10% ammonia has been added.
Tea	All fabrics	Rub with glycerine, then wash with ammonia and water.
Tomato	All fabrics	Wash with water and ammonia. Old stains should be treated like grass stains.
Varnish (nail polish)	All fabrics except rayon	Treat with nail polish remover (acetone), then wash.
Varnish (transparent)	All fabrics	Treat with hot turpentine and alcohol, or with benzine.
Wine (red)	All fabrics	Wash immediately in lukewarm water.

Glossary

Armhole: The space left for the sleeve from the underarm to the shoulder.

Armhole shaping: The decreases made at the beginning of the armhole.

Asterisk: Instructions between two asterisks should be repeated across the whole row. Occasionally the instructions between two asterisks may contain another passage between double asterisks or in brackets followed by an indication of how many times the second operation should be performed.

Bind off: Stitches are bound off so that they do not come undone when a piece of knitting is finished. Some stitches may be bound off while knitting is in progress, for buttonholes, shaping, etc.

Cast on: The operation of making the initial stitches before starting work.

Cast on again: Casting on stitches during a piece of work to increase the width, or to replace stitches which have been bound off.

Chart: A design on graph paper with symbols for the different colours. Used for Jacquard knitting and embroidery.

Darning: The technique of mending holes in finished garments.

Decrease: To eliminate one or more stitches from the needle.

Drop a stitch: Stitches are sometimes dropped on purpose to obtain a lacy effect.

Elongate: To elongate a stitch, wind the wool two or more times around the right-hand needle before inserting the needle in the stitch to be worked. During the next row slip the wound wool off the needle after knitting the stitch and a lacy effect will be obtained.

Eyelets: Decorative small holes which may be used for threading ribbons.

Grosgrain: A corded ribbon of silk, cotton, or artificial fibers, used to strengthen waistbands or to reinforce hems, buttonholes and borders.

Increase: To add one or more stitches to the number of stitches on the needle.

Leaving stitches on a spare needle: One or more stitches may be left on a spare needle or on a stitch holder, to be worked later.

Measurements: The measurements determining the size of a garment.

Pattern or stitch: The effect achieved by repeating a row, or rows.

Pick up a stitch: Picking up a dropped stitch with a crochet hook, or picking up stitches in order to knit a border, such as around the neck.

Pocket lining: The fabric applied to the wrong side of an inset pocket. It is usually of lining material or of a thinner fabric than is used for the garment.

Rejoining: Rejoining the wool to stitches which have been left to one side on a stitch holder.

Repeat: Usually accompanied by "from * to *," or referring to a group of stitches within brackets: the instructions between the asterisks or backets should be repeated the stated number of times.

Right and left edges: The right and left edges of a piece of work facing the knitter at a given moment.

Right side of work: The side of the work which will face out when worn.

Row: All the stitches on the needle. To work a row means to work all the stitches on the left-hand needle.

Selvage: The lateral edges of a piece of work. Unless otherwise indicated in a pattern, the first and last stitch of each row constitute the selvage.

Sides: The sides of a garment are the external edges of the front and the back up to the armhole shaping. To sew the side seam means to stitch front to back along the side edge.

Size: The size of a garment is based on a number of body measurements (height, chest measurement, waist) and the dimensions of the garment can be varied accordingly.

Slip 1, k.1, pass slip stitch over: A method of decreasing at the edge of a piece of knitting or in the middle of a row. Slip one stitch from the left-hand to the right-hand needle without knitting it; knit the following stitch and then lift the slipped stitch over the knitted stitch using the point of the left-hand needle.

Standard: The patterns given in this book are graded according to the degree of expertise required, depending on the stitches used, whether Jacquard patterns are used, complexity of shaping and so on.

Stitch: Each of the closed loops on the needle constitutes one stitch. All the stitches on the needle constitute a row.

Tension: Tension increases or diminishes according to whether you knit with the yarn pulled tight, or with large or small needles. Tension determines the texture and elasticity of knitted fabric – whether it is firm or stretchy. It also determines the size of the finished work. It is important to establish one's individual tension with the yarn one is using by knitting a sample square, to see how the measurements of the finished garment will be affected.

Tension sample: A small square of knitting made so that your own tension (number of stitches and rows to one centimeter or inch) can be calculated accurately. In the patterns in this book the tension sample is always 10cm × 10cm (4″ × 4″).

Twisted: A twisted stitch is knitted through the back of the loop.

Underarm: The top of the side seam and of the sleeve seam.

Wrong side of work: The side facing in when worn.

Yarn: General term given to the fiber used for a piece of knitting.

Yarn back: During knitting, the yarn is brought back when a knit stitch is being worked.

Yarn forward: During knitting, the yarn is brought forward towards the knitter when a purl stitch is being worked after a knit stitch.

Yarn around needle: The yarn is wound once around the needle before a stitch is knitted, either to create an extra stitch (if the new stitch is knitted on the subsequent row) or a small hole (if the new stitch is dropped on the subsequent row).

Index